D1648657

HOW TO DEVELOP A SIX

SUPERSTAR

SELLING

THE MIKE FERRY WAY

FIGURE INCOME IN REAL ESTATE

Dearborn™

Real Estate Education

While a great deal of care has been taken to provide accurate and current information, the ideas, suggestions, general principles and conclusions presented in this text are subject to local, state and federal laws and regulations, court cases and any revisions of same. The reader is thus urged to consult legal counsel regarding any points of law—this publication should not be used as a substitute for competent legal advice.

Publisher: Kathleen A. Welton
Acquisitions Editor: Patrick J. Hogan
Associate Editor: Karen A. Christensen
Senior Project Editor: Jack L. Kiburz
Interior Design: Lucy Jenkins
Cover Design: Design Alliance, Inc.
Cover Photography: Ricky Clay

Published by Real Estate Education Company,
a division of Dearborn Financial Publishing, Inc.

Printed in the United States of America

12 13 14 15 16-06 05 04 03 02

Library of Congress Cataloging-in-Publication Data

Ferry, Mike.
    How to develop a six-figure income in real estate : superstar
selling the Mike Ferry way / Mike Ferry.
        p. cm.
    Includes index.
    ISBN 0-79310-490-4 : $22.50
    1. Real estate business—United States. 2. Real estate agents—
United States. I. Title.
HD255.F47   1992
332.63′24—dc20   92-31396
                                                                          CIP

DEDICATION

To all of those superstars who are always fighting and scratching to make real estate a profession, not just a job. Don't stop battling; it must be done.

TABLE OF CONTENTS

PREFACE

Real estate agents by the thousands from across the country have used the ideas in this book to propel themselves to six-figure incomes. It's not uncommon to see a salesperson's production double within months after starting to use the tools given here. You'll find these steps revolutionary, because they show you how to treat your real estate career as a business. You can then use proven techniques for increasing your productivity.

In *How To Develop a SIX-Figure Income in Real Estate,* you'll learn what forms of prospecting bring results. Prospecting and working on your presentation skills EVERY DAY are the keys to success. It sounds simple, and it works. Building a large customer base guarantees future referrals.

SETTING YOUR GOALS

We make choices in five aspects of our lives: psychological, spiritual, family, physical and financial. Most people never accomplish much in any of those areas, because they have vague goals. Until you become obsessed with what you want from life, your chance of getting it will be minute. You must focus all your energy on the goals you've set.

Begin by taking a piece of paper and writing each area on a separate sheet. Next, list the things you'd like to accomplish in each area. Let your mind go—don't hold back. Don't be surprised if it takes a few days to complete some of these thoughts.

You'll then need to set up an action plan of specific steps for reaching those goals. For instance, if you want to do 100 sales a year, how many listing presentations will you need to make? To get those listing appointments, how many prospects will you have to call each day? Make a commitment to follow your plan, and keep track of the results. Remind yourself daily of your goals and the immediate steps you need to take.

One thing that slows us down is procrastination—a largely unconscious strategy of delay. Researchers say that many chronic procrastinators are afraid of both failure and success. Other slow starters see themselves asserting their authority by not doing anything until they're "ready." Unfortunately, those in the habit of starting late then tend to congratulate themselves on the great job they did at the last minute. Below are some ideas on how to deal with procrastination. If you think they will help you, put them into practice NOW.

1. Try the "five-minute plan" to help you get started. If you've been putting off something that's difficult, commit yourself to working on it for just five minutes. Chances are you'll stick with it and keep going. Another method is to do the easy part of a job first to get a sense of accomplishment.
2. Break your patterns. If you're watching television when you should be doing something else, at least quit watching television. Even if you can't get going on your project, you're changing your habit.
3. Ask for help. The most productive people don't take on every job. They know how to delegate and when to ask for assistance.
4. Make sure you understand the task. Often we avoid something just because we're unclear on how to proceed.
5. If you really get clicking on a project, stay with it as long as the energy is there.

After reading *How To Develop a SIX-Figure Income in Real Estate,* you'll be so excited that procrastination should no longer be a concern. You'll then know how to make your real estate career into a growing business. Someday I hope to meet each of you, perhaps at one of my seminars, and to hear your success story.

—Mike Ferry

CHAPTER 1

How the Superstar System Works

"Find out what everybody else is doing and then simply do the opposite."

—Earl Nightingale

Earl Nightingale knew that great salespeople are basically different from those who are not so great. It's not a matter of just being better organized, a little harder working, or luckier; what they have going for them is an approach to thinking and working that is vastly different from that of the normal real estate agent.

Do you have the courage to be unique? It would require tremendous self-confidence in your ability to solve problems and the strength not to run from difficult situations when they occur.

At age 25, I was Earl Nightingale's national training director. I left to sell residential real estate and averaged 26 transactions per month for the next two years. For the past 14 years I've been a real estate trainer—and some of my ideas have been controversial:

- In 1981 I advised agents to stop doing floor time and quit using classified ads.

- In 1982 I came out against farming. By that time, real estate agents had passed out enough pumpkins to last everyone 47 lifetimes.
- In 1983 I told agents that open houses are an excuse for not really working.

You wouldn't expect much response from these ideas, would you, since they all go against commonly taught industry practices? But remember what Earl Nightingale said? Maybe it works.

Do you think that thoughts like those above help produce top agents? Everyone said we were charging too much when we held our first Action Workshop in 1980. Since then over 20,000 agents have benefitted from them. Then in 1985 we held our first superstar retreat. At last year's, 3,000 agents came for four days. By the way, their average annual income was SIX figures.

WHY IT WORKS

What I've discovered is that most real estate training is based on old-fashioned marketing ideas that don't work. Real estate is a direct-sales job, and many agents don't recognize that—or they aren't willing to do the prospecting work it takes. Look at it this way: Ours is the only industry in which you can be totally unproductive and still win a plaque, simply because your listing sold. Real estate offices are practically adult day-care centers for some agents.

One lady who came to a seminar of mine was her company's top producer. She had completed 11 transactions the previous year, for a total volume of over $30 million. I asked her if she was part-time. Why had she done only 11 deals?

Gross sales volume is not a fair measuring stick of people's productivity. Instead, we should look at the *annual number of transactions*. It's true you can do one big deal and get a plaque, but if you put together 100 deals a year, you'll be happy with your income no matter what the average sales price is.

Through this book, I can teach you specific strategies for accomplishing a SIX-figure level of production. But that means I'll have to tell you the truth, not what you want to hear. To begin with, it's a mistake to think that doing paperwork, talking with other agents, showing homes to unqualified buyers, holding open houses or doing floor time is productive.

What *is* productive is listing and selling homes. To do so, you must constantly be asking prospects if they would like to list or sell. When I was an agent, I did cold doors because there was nothing else to do. When you're out there cold-door knocking, three questions can quickly gauge a prospect's motivation:

- "When do you plan on moving?"
- "How long have you been here?"
- "If you were to move, where would you go?"

After hearing responses to these questions, you'll know what the prospect is planning to do and whether or not you should spend any more time with him. In the chapters that follow, we'll look more closely at how these questions qualify sellers and allow you to present yourself as a professional.

Most agents believe they must first become friends with sellers—establish rapport, and "bond" with them. Right? Wrong, wrong, wrong! That worked in the 1960s and '70s, but today's market is different. Sellers are looking for agents who perform—period. A real estate professional should be like a doctor: He or she is basically there to take care of a problem. There's no time for "bonding" in this business today.

DOES IT WORK IN ALL MARKETS?

As I write this, we are in a period of slow sales and sagging prices in many areas of the country. Superstar agents think that's great, and here's why: As the number of deals in an area diminishes, the number of salespeople operating in that marketplace will be shrinking even faster. People will be leaving the business. More important, a good percentage of those who are left are tense, terrified and just not working. They are "waiting for the market to improve."

That's bad for them, but good for you. Realistically, the time for you to succeed has never been better. There's an abundance of sellers who have to sell and a lot of buyers who have to buy. Yet there are only a handful of superstars who are out there working every day and taking advantage of the situation.

One thing you need to do during slow times is work as quickly as possible to build listing inventories. Now, someone (obviously not a superstar) might say, "But Mike, listings aren't selling; why do I need more of them?" Let's take a look at the obvious. When the market slows down and fewer listings are selling, we still have to realize that *some* listings are moving. Somebody who has listings is getting paid, right?

If you have one listing, what are the odds of it selling in your marketplace if there are 1,000 listings? But if you have 20 listings, your chance of one selling is at least 20 times greater. The more listings you have, the better chance you have that somebody is going to sell one of them. And when the market changes—which it will—you'll make more money with all those listings than you ever thought was possible!

GETTING STARTED—20 TECHNIQUES OF THE SUPERSTARS

Successful people are masters of the basics. When you consistently use techniques that work, business will keep flowing in. The basic requirements for agents are strong prospecting and presentation skills. Superstars prospect a minimum of three hours every day. They also are masters of their presentation, which makes the close a very simple process. Look, objections only arise as a result of a weak presentation. Are you as good in these areas as you should be?

Because simpler is better at a listing presentation, the two most important questions are:

- *"What is your motivation to move?"* If they aren't motivated, it won't sell in today's market. Don't waste your time on such people.
- *"What price do you want?"* Unrealistic pricing will keep a home in MLS until it burns down.

In this book I'll show you how to apply these concepts so you can become more efficient—and earn more money. Does this system work? Tens of thousands of agents use it. About 25,000 agents have been to my superstar retreats, and some of them do more than 300 deals a year.

How To Develop a SIX-Figure Income in Real Estate contains techniques these top agents use. It's packed with basic scripts, prospecting strategies and powerful ideas that will propel your production skyward.

In Chapter 12, you'll find out how these agents put to work the strategies I've outlined here. Many good agents have seen their income double within months after implementing the ideas in this book. Even using just one or two can make a big difference. But the question is, are you willing to pay the price—not in terms of working longer hours, but by holding to a plan that is designed to help you achieve your goals?

In this chapter I'm going to give you an overview of innovative approaches for reaching real estate sales excellence in the 1990s. Today's market brings new realities, and agents who want to be superstars must respond to it with new ideas. Here are 20 strategies used by some of the best producers in the United States and Canada:

Idea #1 —Learn To Run Real Estate as if It Were a Business

We would all agree that the primary purpose of a business is to provide superior service to customers while also making a profit. Yet many agents are frustrated to find that at the end of the year, they don't have enough money left to pay taxes. Despite their income level, they are not running a profitable business. Is this your situation?

Here's what I suggest: Cut whatever you're spending on advertising, personal promotion or gifts by half—and immediately pay yourself the difference. Then ask yourself:

1. How would your customer rate your service?
2. Are you retaining the profit you want?

Treat your company as a business first, second and third. Make only business decisions. Don't get involved in anything that does not increase production, help the staff or increase profits. As an agent, you may not like some of the decisions you may have to reach as a business owner. Some of these tough—but necessary—matters will be raised in the rest of the 20 ideas in this chapter.

Set specific standards for your staff and enforce them. Why? Because too often agents have either no standards or low standards for productivity, the quality of people in their office and profits. As a result, they don't attain greatness in any of these three areas. Monitor your staff continuously. "Bug" them to perform in order to reach goals. Finally, don't become emotionally attached to your staff; build business rapport, not social rapport.

Idea #2 — Learn To Initiate Change, Not React to It

We spend most of our time reacting to others, don't we? But if you stick to your business plan rather than getting upset at your assistant, the other agent or the title company, then you'll make more money. Now, this won't happen overnight. Many agents can go from anger to elation in one morning, for this is an emotional business. But with practice, you'll be able to stay with what you need to do to be more productive, instead of letting things you can't control affect you.

Remember, your productivity depends 100 percent on your attitude and skills, not on what one prospect says to you. Put the two to work and you'll reach whatever goals you've set.

Initiating change means studying what is happening in real estate and then altering your business accordingly. Begin by asking, "Where does my business come from? Can I duplicate what I've done in the past to be successful today?" It's not 1988 any more, and a different climate demands new methods. We'll get into them as we go along.

Idea #3 — Never Need a Deal, but Always Want One

Desperation is the downfall of all success and all wealth. Don't allow yourself to be desperate, even when you are. It's simple—change your thinking. If you're desperate, then buyers and sellers control you. You'll agree to an unrealistic price or an overly aggressive marketing program in order to get the listing. Or worse, you'll be wasting your time chauffeuring buyers who might not qualify for a loan.

Do attorneys allow someone else to tell them how to run their business? If you're a professional, when you walk into a house, the owners should be thrilled you're there. *You* decide if you want to list the property then—they shouldn't be qualifying you. Because you're the professional, you won't make unbusinesslike decisions about who you want to work with.

Instead of telling owners how beautiful their carpets are to "build rapport," you'll be following your business plan. You'll find out how motivated to sell they are, and then you'll tell them what price and terms they need in order to do that. And if you stick with this system, you'll have so many prospects that you won't need every single deal.

Idea #4 — Price and Motivation Are the Only Issues in Listing Property

Nothing else counts. Of course, the higher a seller's motivation, the lower the listing price. Low-motivation sellers are just the opposite; don't waste your time on them—another company can list them. Try saying this: "Mr. and Mrs. Seller, a number of companies in town specialize in homes that take a long time to sell. Why don't I have one of them give you a call?" Otherwise, you will be in an unbusinesslike situation. If you work only with motivated sellers, you'll make more money, right?

Idea #5 — Always Tell the Truth Throughout Your Presentation

This is important. Agents are tempted to veer from the truth when they don't have enough prospects and need a listing. But don't make the mistake of listing a nonmotivated seller by saying, "I'll try to get the price you want." Tell your sellers the facts about market conditions. Even though they may not want to hear them, they need to.

If you come to a listing presentation prepared and always tell the truth, you'll be a better salesperson than if you rely on fast talk. Let your customer know that you are telling the whole truth about yourself, your company, the marketplace and all other existing conditions. You will lose some listings and sales because you've told the truth. But isn't it a better long-range policy to maintain your integrity?

Remember, at the base of every problem is a lie. Look for the lie, rather than trying to invent a solution. What you're actually doing is developing a sensitivity to the needs of your prospects. Then you'll be able to listen to their viewpoint and quickly tell when they are open to your presentation. If you know you've done your best, you won't pressure yourself with unrealistic expectations. And whatever you do, don't be attached to the outcome.

Idea #6 — Never Spend More Than 20 Minutes on a Listing Presentation

Only go once to a prospect's house. Give it your best shot, and then go on to the next one. Why wouldn't you spend more than 20 minutes with prospects? Either they want to sell or they don't. Of course, you can't do this unless you have lots of prospects. Here's how it works.

1. Have your assistant call to set up an appointment and ask the following qualifying questions:
    *   Are you planning on listing your home with Mike when he comes?
    *   Where are you moving to?
    *   How soon must you move?
    *   What price do you want?
    *   How much do you owe on your home?
    *   Do you plan on selling by yourself?
    *   Can you help the buyer with financing?
        After these questions are answered, you might not want the listing. If so, cancel the appointment.
2. Mail or deliver your marketing plan, a list of references and promotional items.
3. Always call back within a few days. At that time you should ask:
    *   How did you pick the price you want?
    *   Would you think about lowering your price?
        After you've heard their answers, either confirm or cancel the appointment.
4. Show up on time, and give your listing presentation.

If you have guts, also do the following:

5. Before the appointment, mail or deliver your Comparable Market Analysis (CMA) with your recommended listing price circled in red.
6. Ask the prospects to come to your office. Why? Because it saves time and gives you more control of the situation.

Idea #7 — If You Don't Use Idea #6, Have a Biweekly Status Report Delivered to the Seller

On it simply list the following facts:

*   Number of homes sold since the last report in your area
*   Number of homes sold year-to-date in your area and the average price

- Number of homes for sale in your area when you listed
- Number of homes for sale now
- Number of homes that failed to sell year-to-date
- My recommendation regarding price: $_____

In reality, price is the only reason a property won't sell. Location, terms and condition are not the issue. Sending a report like this makes a lot of people mad, but being mad is not the issue, either. I'd rather the seller be mad than me, because that means we're working on lowering the price.

Idea #8 — Develop a High-Impact Prospecting Program, and Use It Three Hours a Day

Agents have more control over results when doing high-impact prospecting. What does high-impact prospecting mean? Some examples are cold calls, cold doors, calling on FSBOs and expired listings, interoffice and direct referrals, past client contacts and mail-outs with phone follow-up. On the other hand, low-impact prospecting has less predictable results. If you rely on open houses, floor time, occasional mailers and traditional farming to get your commissions, you'll never hit the SIX-figure mark.

Don't be a "secret" agent. Instead, start building your mailing list of friends, clients and "spheres of influence," and mail to them every four to six weeks. Superstars reach up to 25,000 names in a few years. These mailings simply remind your "people farm" that you're still in the real estate business. If people know what you do, they'll support you. Here's a bonus benefit: An agent who is prospecting for listings will find buyers as well.

Idea #9 — Add This Addendum to Your Listing Contract: "Seller Agrees To Meet with Agent at Agent's Office Every Two Weeks until Property Sells To Discuss Price"

You're in an environment where major newspapers print articles advising consumers to ask agents to cut their commissions, commit to lots of ads and open houses, and take 90-day listings. If something isn't done to balance these forces, the way real estate is sold could change.

So whenever a newspaper runs articles damaging to agents, I suggest they write the editor to complain about the articles, and further state that they will never run real estate classifieds in that publication again.

Idea #10 — Put Another Addendum in Listing Contracts: "Seller Agrees To Reimburse Agent All Advertising Costs at Close of Escrow or Cancellation of Listing"

You'll find this keeps sellers from automatically coming at you with a list of demands. Taking this stand is hard, because agents often are conditioned to be whipping posts. Remember, if you do what's right professionally, you're in control of your business. Because people respect someone who can make a decision, there will be less resistance than you think.

Idea #11 — Hire an Assistant

The assistant's only job would be to (1) follow up on all your leads and ask the questions listed in Idea #6 or (2) prospect for you all the time by phone. This allows you to spend more of your time at appointments to list and sell property, which means more time to make money, right? Having an assistant is crucial to keeping you on track and not letting you get off the schedule you've set. This is important: Delegate everything you can to your support team. Then set an exact daily schedule for what you want to accomplish, and check it every hour of the day. Concentrate on priorities. Remember, even if you don't have an assistant, you really do—except *you're* doing the work an assistant should do.

Idea #12 — Work FSBOs and Expired Listings

You need to talk to people who are going to buy or sell a home, and not to the other agents in your office. Here's an easy way to get an appointment: Tell them how many of your listings you've sold in the last 30 days. If you're a superstar, they'll be impressed with the results and want to talk with you. Many people in the business never prospect at all. But for top agents, prospecting is always a priority. An agent calling on five expired listings each day should get one new listing daily.

Idea #13 — Create a Simple, Effective, Inexpensive Personal Marketing Campaign

I'll give you some guidelines that work. Don't spend a lot until you have it. Talk one-on-one with prospects first; then develop a brochure when you have the money to do so.

Also, start a press-release farm. How do you do this? It's simple: Make a list of editors in your area, and send them a press release every two weeks on something noteworthy you've done. This works great, because you'll start getting free publicity. But remember, the best method of personal marketing is a "sold" sign in the front yard of one of your listings.

Idea #14 — Stop Trying To Make Your Systems Perfect

If you're consistently having a problem with time management, don't put too much pressure on yourself to go from a bad system to a great one overnight. The transformation to being a good time manager is going to take four to six months, so keep working at it. If you work diligently each day to improve, I guarantee you'll achieve your goal.

For most agents, it makes sense to computerize to keep track of leads. If you don't computerize, your assistant will have to record your leads on index cards. Either way, you'll need to establish a tickler system so you know when it's time to contact each lead again. Depending on how warm the lead is, your assistant should call or mail a note as often as every ten days. FSBOs fit into this category, since they could decide to list at any time.

Your longer-term prospects usually come from cold doors or cold calls. Have your assistant phone them monthly and say, "Mike asked me to give you a call to make sure you've been receiving the mail that we've sent. He also wanted to know if you've moved up your targeted date for listing/buying."

If you're computerized, a list should be on your desk each morning showing the people you have to contact that day. If you miss them by phone, send a computer-generated letter telling them that you called and when you'll call again.

Computers are wonderful—and also can be a pain. That's why you need to hire a computer expert to set up your system, rather than spending the time to learn it yourself. After all, your job is to fill your time with listings, prospects and leads, right? If you don't do that, even the most sophisticated computer system won't be very helpful.

Idea #15 — Create a Schedule for the Next 90 Days

You're going to be working from seven to ten-plus hours per day, five days per week. Your time should be organized like this:

1. High-impact prospecting, 20 percent
2. Listing presentations, 30 percent
3. Negotiating offers and contracts on your listings, 20 percent
4. Getting price reductions, 20 percent
5. Personal promotion, 10 percent

Idea #16 — Set Up an Intensive Price-Reduction Campaign ASAP

It is your obligation to get the highest price for the seller. But sellers must understand that the market is competitive, and a price reduction will make their house stand out. How do you accomplish your goal? Tell your listings: "I have made a terrible mistake and am sorry. I wasn't strong enough on price when you listed." Then offer four possible solutions:

1. Reduce the price 20 percent.
2. Raise the commission 1 percent, to get the attention of other agents.
3. Extend the listing another 90 days, in hopes that the home will appreciate during that time and then sell.
4. Take the listing back.

Quit asking for small price reductions, such as from $198,500 to $196,500. Ask for a 20 percent reduction. If you get less—say, 10 percent—you're still better off than you were before.

It doesn't matter how many price reductions you've asked for already. This may sound extreme, but request another one. Why?

Because you'll sell more listings when the prices are lower. If the seller's motivation is as high as you would like to believe it is, then ask again. Assuming the owner is truly interested in selling his or her property, then you are serving his or her needs by suggesting a price reduction.

Idea #17 — Get Your Assistant To Evaluate the Market

A monthly evaluation will help you see where you should concentrate your efforts. You can get data from your local board or from title companies, and look for trends. For instance, if you find that even well-priced condos aren't selling in your area, then don't list any.

Idea #18 — Support Those People Who Are Willing To Support You

You can do this in several ways. For instance, pick and stay with one title company, mortgage lender and personal promotion firm. And don't always be looking for the best deal.

One of the most difficult issues is how to meet family demands and increase your earnings at the same time. Why not sit down with your spouse and children and share with them the goals that you've set? Tell them exactly what you'll have to do to accomplish them, including how much time it will take. More important, show them the benefits they'll have when you achieve those goals.

Good communication is a key to success both with your customers and with your family. If you follow up on your intentions by scheduling time with your spouse and children, you'll have their support for your business, too. There is more to life than being a real estate salesperson. But to make this work, you'll have to learn other skills. In the office, you'll need to quit procrastinating, stick with your plan and learn to delegate.

You'll have to learn to say no to bad listings and nonproductive buyers, because they take time away from what you need to do in today's market—and that is prospect. If you're prospecting all the time, there is no reason for you to take a listing that you know is not going to sell. Increase the number of contacts that you make daily while prospecting, and say no to those that don't make sense.

Idea #19 — Constantly Spend Creative Time Looking For Ways To Find Buyers for Your Listings

Everyone likes to sell his or her own listings, right? You pick up both commissions, and it's so much easier to deal with the other agent when *you* are the other agent.

If you're not marketing your listings to the top 100 agents in your town, then start doing so right away. Also, make sure that whatever marketing you're doing has the potential to bring results, not just satisfy the seller.

To be a superstar, you're going to spend most of your time doing high-impact prospecting. This is great, because it brings you both buyers and sellers. How do you do it? Start with a marketing campaign to tenants—you'll find prime buying candidates for your own listings. Another good technique, where appropriate, is to show buyers your own listings first. And finally, get yourself a lot of well-priced listings. The greater the number, the higher the likelihood that some will get sold.

Idea #20 — Develop an Intensive Personal Development Program—Starting Today

First of all, go to seminars. Why? Because they keep you up to date and stimulated with new ideas. And new ideas mean that you won't go stale on the same old techniques; they challenge you to think fresh and think SIX. Next, spend an hour each morning reading. It's a great way to wake up and get excited. Also start a "people-reading" program. Quit talking about sports and the weather; find out what makes others successful. Spend time with people smarter than you are. Each year successful people grow in terms of knowledge—and income—by 20 percent.

If you listen to tapes in the car on your way to appointments, they help you stay on track. Why? Because your desire and creativity increase when you feed them motivational thoughts. "But Mike, I don't have time to listen to motivational tapes. Do I have to?" It's true that most people are too busy being busy. It's a vicious circle: They don't have time to learn how to become more productive. But yes, you have to schedule in time to do so. For instance, try setting up a monthly brainstorming session with other top agents; you'll help each other come up with new ideas and solve problems.

PREPARING YOURSELF

To implement just the first ten ideas here will take 12 to 18 months—and the next ten ideas are even harder. But you're not going anywhere now, are you? Can you wait two years to get the income and recognition that you want? Start by setting specific goals for yourself. How does this work? First you're going to develop an action plan. Write down your business and personal goals. Then list all the benefits you'll enjoy when you achieve each goal. Share your plans with someone else, and review them every day to stay focused. Ask yourself each day, "How much do I want it?"

What will motivate you to put all 20 ideas into action? If you get so excited about yourself you can't stand it, and every day you're working toward your goals, then this book has made a difference.

Distractions, other people and negative thoughts are obstacles to your goals. Okay, so what can you do about them? If you review your goals daily, you can eliminate some of these influences. Is the goal realistic? Can you clearly see yourself obtaining the results? You must become almost fanatical in your singleness of purpose. You have to want to achieve the goals you've set so badly that you can virtually see, touch, smell and taste them.

This isn't so hard as you might think. For example, look at the financial side of the plan. Have you clearly and realistically defined what you want to earn this year? Have you broken down a monthly, weekly and daily goal for yourself? Have you identified all the activities you'll have to do each day to achieve this? Believe me, you can't overplan for success.

I'm assuming that you've written a detailed business plan that tells you exactly what to expect, and also exactly what you're going to do. Let me tell you a secret: The key to business planning is not only the details you write, but also the fact that you commit to the plan every day. This means you're going to take action every day on all the activities that are necessary to complete the goals you've set.

Are you monitoring activities and results every day toward the achievement of your goals? What are the obvious difficulties that could get in the way? Do you have contingency plans to overcome these obstacles if they occur?

Most real estate agents make a living, and there's nothing wrong with that. But did you know that only 3 or 4 percent of all agents in this country make any real money? You are free to choose and can improve yourself one thought at a time. Concentrate on the positives, not the negatives. When the market is turbulent and the economy is fluctuating, and everybody around you is telling you why you can't do it, it takes a lot of courage and discipline to remain positive.

"Okay, Mike. Everybody talks about positive thinking, but most real estate agents aren't superstars." If you start by changing your attitude, you'll upgrade what you do daily. Superstars believe they can do it no matter what; and self-belief is a powerful thing. These people believe 100 percent in their company and their product, but most important, in themselves. When you have such strong self-belief, it shows to your clients and wins their confidence. And we all know that means more money.

Superstars are also risk takers. Calling on an expired listing is a risky situation, right? Maybe. But the higher the risk, the higher the potential payoff. Expand your awareness of what you can do, and learn to handle success. It's a fact that most people are never overly success- ful, simply because they can't imagine themselves earning that much money. To do so, they also would have to change all their habits and learn the techniques that make a great salesperson. Do you want to be a superstar agent? By learning the basics, paying the price and changing your habits, you can choose to become a top producer.

You can spot superstars because they look, act, talk and walk like the achievers they are. But you don't have to go out and buy a new wardrobe to start. It doesn't cost much to be well-groomed, nor is it expensive to keep your desktop clear.

If you want to become a superstar, if you want to develop that SIX-figure income, you can. There is absolutely nothing standing between you and your dreams except your fears. So how do you prepare yourself? First of all, you have to establish goals on several levels: annually, quarterly, monthly, weekly and daily. Since you're a real estate agent, what is your basic goal? To list and sell property, right? Everything that you do should result in one of those two items.

You have to decide how many transactions you want to be involved in. Let's say that you want to be involved in 48 this year. Okay, that means you need to close 12 deals a quarter, four a month or one a week. That doesn't sound impossible. Only one deal a week. But what do you have to do to be involved in one deal a week? You have to talk to at least 100 people to get one deal, either a listing or a sale. This is called prospecting. You will have to organize your day so that you speak to at least 20 people about listing or selling property. Some will be cold doors, others will be cold phone calls and others will be FSBOs and expired listings.

"But Mike, I want to be a selling agent." Okay, you're still going to have to speak to at least 100 people per week in order to get one buyer. But I have a question for you: Why would you want to give up half of the business by working only listings or sales? Both parts are integral portions of the business. You can make money from either side, so why not make it from both sides of a transaction? If you're only working one side of the street, you won't be making all of the money that you could.

Another way to be prepared for the opportunity is to dress as though you're successful. Take a look around the office. How are most of the other agents dressed? In a casual fashion, right? Okay, lesson number one: See what most of the other agents do, and don't do it. If they're dressed in a casual fashion, you should be dressed in a tie or business suit. Why? Because the average, coffee-drinking agent is only making $10 per hour. If you want to emulate someone, emulate the top producer. Emulate the professional. Emulate the successful!

However, there's a little problem: If a person is successful, he or she won't be spending a lot of time in the office. You might only see them once a week, if that. So what else does that tell you? If you want to be successful, stay out of the office. You won't be selling much real estate to other agents, and who will you find in the office? Other agents. You have to go out and look for business.

Don't worry, I'm going to tell you how to do that. I'll give you a systematic and complete plan. If you follow this plan, my plan, the Superstar Plan, you can make any amount of money you want.

I realize that most of your goals will not be related to money. Quite a few of them will be of a personal nature. I have no way of knowing what those might be, except in the broadest terms. Sure, you might want more time with your family, or more time to take vacations.

What all of you will have in common, though, is that you want to make a certain amount of money. If you're going to work 40 hours a week, don't you want it to be as productive as possible? Sure, you do! So read and follow the instructions I give you, and regardless of what your goals might be, you will be able to achieve them.

Are you ready for success? Are you ready to become a superstar? Are you ready to achieve your goals? Good. Let's get started!

Hi Mike,

You've made me over a million dollars and I probably haven't told you so! Yes, it's true—in the last five years, all I've done is use your simple time-management system, and because of it I've earned an additional one million dollars in commissions to myself.

It started for me in 1981, when I attended your program and you outlined that simple yet precise method of getting more done in less time. I guess I was ready for something, because I remember sitting there that day and wondering why I hadn't heard this before and why I hadn't figured it out on my own.

Marcy and I have no other way to say thank you than to say thank you. As you know, in the last five or six years we've been able to dramatically improve our life-styles, develop a sound personal investment program and really start to enjoy life.

Mike, I've told you about some of my financial difficulties, and believe me, even when you didn't know you were doing it, you've turned our lives around. Now, we're really looking forward to the future—not only to the great things that we can do, but to the fun we can have. Let us know how we can help return the tremendous favor you have bestowed upon us.

Calvin G.

CHAPTER 2

The Superstar Way to Time Management

Time management is the single most misunderstood topic for real estate salespeople. Time management, or the lack of it, has caused more real estate sales deaths than anything else. You have opportunities to practice and perfect presentations through rehearsal and repetition; you only get one chance per prospect to utilize it productively.

The topics that are covered in this chapter are:

- The Importance of Time Management
- Working Less and Earning More
- Weekly Activities of the Superstar
- How To Fill Out a Weekly Planner

By carefully reading, understanding and following the instructions listed in this chapter, you will be on your way to becoming a superstar.

THE IMPORTANCE OF TIME MANAGEMENT

You're excited! This is your first "real" day in the real estate business. You have your license, you've been through the sales training course for new real estate agents that your company sponsors, and you're ready to go out there to list and sell. You're going to be the top producing agent this month! You're going to shine brighter than anyone ever has or ever will! Well . . .

You drive up to your office with pride. There's a small lump in your throat when you see the sign that says "Banana Realty," with that great gold banana as the logo. That's something to be proud of; why, your last employer didn't even *have* a logo!

Brimming with enthusiasm, you enter the front door and go to your desk. After you sit down, you notice a coffee cup on your desk with your name on it, a present from the company. You look around and see several other agents sitting at their desks with their feet up drinking coffee from their "banana" cups. "They seem friendly enough," you tell yourself. They have all said hello and smiled. "Maybe this is what I should be doing," you think.

Wrong, wrong, wrong! If you want to be a superstar, if you dare to Think SIX, it is wrong. The only thing that the "banana" cup should be used for is pencils, or maybe a plant. But whatever it's used for, it should not be coffee. You're not going to be in the office enough to put it to use.

The biggest advantage of being a real estate sales agent is that you're an independent contractor. You set your own hours, you determine what you're going to do with your day, and you ultimately determine how much money you're going to make. Aren't those some of the reasons you went into real estate?

All of those little freedoms, and the freedom of being an independent contractor, provide great opportunities. However, the same freedom that allows you to decide how much money you're going to make can also spell poverty. You have to be the master of your own time if you're going to make the money you want. If you don't manage your time, nobody else will.

Just a comment on the value of time for even a mediocre real estate agent (please note, not a "sales" agent). A real estate agent who makes the median of $22,500 a year makes an average of about $10 per hour.

If this same agent spends two hours a day in the office drinking coffee and staring at a closed MLS book, then that coffee has cost the agent $20. That's pretty expensive coffee. I hope they used golden beans when they made it, because that's all the gold this agent will see. If you're going to be a superstar, you cannot afford to spend time in the office drinking coffee.

There are two kinds of people in the real estate business: There are real estate people or agents, and there are real estate *sales*people or agents. What's the difference? It's all in how they spend their time. Real estate people spend their time in the office drinking coffee and hoping to get extra floor time; real estate *sales*people spend their time out of the office looking for business and trying to reduce their floor time. Who do you think will be the superstar?

If you think your time is worth $10 per hour and you don't want to earn any more than that, then waste your time in the office. But if you think your time is worth $100 per hour, then determine how you invest your time by managing it, and you will be further along your way to becoming a superstar.

By the way, if you do decide your time is worth $100 per hour and you manage your time accordingly, you will make $200,000 per year, which will definitely put you in the superstar category! Now that you're on your way to that SIX-figure income, a few words about the greatest time robbers of them all are in order. Clients all go to Client University, which is affectionately known by all of its graduates as 'CU'. That's exactly what clients will tell you when *they* manage *your* time and the situation, rather than you.

Upon entry to good ol' CU, the first course reminds clients that you're paid by commission when a sale occurs. They are trained to regard your time as not being valuable and to look upon it as their own. Nothing is further from the truth!

You must control your own time in order to control how much money you make. You control your time by deciding what is important and scheduling it accordingly. You schedule time for clients and have them fit their schedules to yours. That's effective time management.

There will be specific instructions a little later in this chapter regarding the "how to's" of time management. But whatever you do, don't forget about good ol' CU.

WORKING LESS AND
EARNING MORE

Working less and earning more—what a novel concept! Can it be a reality? Don't you have to put in the big hours to earn the big bucks? Don't superstars have to put in supertime? The answer to the last question is yes.

I can see you now. You're saying "I got you, Mike. All of this superstar stuff is just so we'll put in more time for the broker," and so on. Nothing could be further from the truth. Supertime is time that has been organized and managed so that it will be the most productive. You must realize that money, productivity and time management are interrelated. The person who controls your time controls how much money you make.

Who can control your time better than you? If you don't begin to create your own supertime schedule, you'll find that everyone—from your clients to your broker and your fellow agents—will be trying to steal your time. If they're stealing your time, they're stealing money out of your pocket. Do you get the idea that I think time management is of the utmost importance if you're to be a superstar? You're right, I do. So let's get down to some nuts and bolts of time management.

You need to determine where your time is currently being spent. The only way to do that is to keep a daily record of your time for the next two weeks. When you record your time, do it hour by hour, rather than just listing what you did during the day. Be honest about it. There's no use doing this if you aren't going to accurately record what you're doing. The only person you're going to fool is yourself. The only one you will hurt is yourself. By not giving a true account of your time during these two weeks, you may actually be stealing money out of your own pocket. This record is nothing more than a tool to help you discover where your time is actually going. By knowing that, you can make better use of it by eliminating or reorganizing activities.

For example, let's say you have to go across town to the same closing office three times during the course of a day. Wouldn't it be better to make one trip? Of course it would. "But Mike, the closing office is just five minutes away." Sure, it's just five minutes away, but why does it always take you 30 minutes to go there and back just to drop off some papers? The answer is that you get sidetracked into doing nonproductive "things." Nonproductive things are those that have very little or nothing to do with the listing and selling of real estate. Every activity that's not concerned with these items is stealing money from you, because it's stealing your time.

Keep the daily hour-by-hour record and keep it honest. Trust me, it will help you make more money. And we did agree that's why you originally got into real estate, right? As you look at your record, you'll suddenly become aware that you seem to be duplicating your efforts— i.e., you're doing the same sort of activity several times a day for short periods. That's not the most productive use of your time. That's not supertime. That's not the way to work if you think you're worth $100 per hour.

What should you do? Consolidate your time into blocks so it's more productive for you. Does it make sense to make three separate trips out of the office to preview property when you could consolidate them into one trip? "But Mike, I'm different. If I don't do something as soon as I think of it, I'll forget to do it."

Yes, you're different; you're also poor. If your way keeps you poor and my way earns you more money, whose way should you follow? Pretty easy answer, isn't it? Don't worry, you'll learn how to remember your errands and how to make more money. Just pay attention.

Do all of your office work at one time. Sounds easy enough; it even makes sense. In fact, that's the way you've tried to do it. However . . . That "however" has to do with the amount of time you've devoted to office work and when you've devoted that time. Are you ever able to get your office work done, or is there always a little something you've left undone even after spending three or four hours at the office?

Just how productive were those three or four hours? Well, you were able to solve Mary's babysitting problem, and you were able to recommend a good mechanic to Fred for his car, and . . . and . . . and. The point is that you were not doing your office work.

It's fine to help others, but do that when you're on your own time, not time you've scheduled for work. If you've spent three hours at the office and only really worked one hour, then you're wasting time. If you think your time is worth $100 per hour, then Mary and Fred have just hit you for $200. Are you beginning to get the picture?

Once again, consolidate your time into blocks. Identify what you need to accomplish, and organize yourself so you're doing the same task for several hours or until the task is completed. Do all of your errands at one time; get your office work done, all of it; preview properties at one time (don't try to do your errands and preview properties at the same time); and above all, DO NOT start one task until another is done.

Concentrate on your priorities. As a real estate sales agent, you have two main priorities, and only two: the listing and selling of property.

You must think about what you want to achieve. Earl Nightingale said, "You become what you think about most of the time." So think about the listing and selling of property. Don't concentrate on your or other people's problems; they will just get in the way of your success. Remember Fred and Mary? They managed to take $200 from you, and you did not complete your office work. If you want to make SIX figures, avoid nonsense when you're in the office.

Since the listing and selling of property is your priority, it makes sense to delegate less important activities to others. That's sometimes difficult to do, because you think you'll lose control. You don't want to trust other people with your deal, with your baby. And if you were to delegate to others, you wouldn't be able to watch over your deal for the next 45 days. Hogwash!

Once you have the signed contracts, let the specialists do what they're best at and get out of their way. How many transactions were you involved in last year? Twelve, maybe 15? How many transactions did the closing officer that you use handle last year? One hundred? Two hundred? More? The point is, who is better equipped to supervise the closing process, you or the closing officer? Get out of the way and let the closing officer take care of it.

"But Mike, I really care about my clients. I want to make sure everything is going well." Great. Then get out of the way and let the specialists do their jobs. If you were a doctor with a general practice and you had a friend who needed brain surgery, you wouldn't insist upon performing the surgery yourself. You would call in a brain specialist.

It's the same thing with real estate. Your job is to list and sell property. The closing officer's job is to collect and verify documents as they apply to the sale of property. Once you have a signed contract, turn it over to a closing officer—preferably the same one every time. Find a closing officer you feel comfortable with and make the following proposition: "I will have about 40 [or 20, or 30] deals this year that will need your services. I would like to use you exclusively; however, if there are any problems, solve them. Don't call me to solve them. I will contact you each week on Wednesday morning for an update on each deal. Okay?" Believe me, you'll get the closing officer's cooperation, and it will free you to do what you do best: list and sell more property, which will make you more money. This is great stuff, and it works.

I recently went to lunch with a friend who is making about $70,000 a year selling real estate. Not bad, but certainly not what he could be making. As we talked, he mentioned that he needed to see the financial officer of a local savings and loan. I asked him if he was buying more property and he said no, he was doing this for a client.

"John, why don't you send them to a mortgage banker to help them arrange a loan? He must be more aware of prevailing rates and special loans than you are."

"But Mike, I just wouldn't feel that I was giving my clients the proper service if I did that."

"John, if you would turn it over to a mortgage banker, a specialist, you would be doing your clients a greater service. As a result, you would have more time to list and sell houses, which is what you do best, and you would make more money."

John's wife was with us, and the last statement really caught her attention.

"John, you would make more money if you were to delegate a little? Would that really work?"

Well, John did get a little uncomfortable. He knew that if he were to delegate responsibilities to escrow officers, mortgage bankers, title companies, termite inspectors, etc., he would have more time to make more money. I don't have a doubt John could become a superstar. No question about it, he has the skill; he just needs to delegate in order to work less and earn more money.

Do you know why some real estate agents don't feel motivated? It's because they don't have a daily plan. Oh, sure, they might have a daily appointment book; but it's blank, or it has 'Lunch with Mike' listed for noon. A book like that really makes you want to get out of bed in the morning and attack the day, doesn't it? No, it does not. It makes you want to stay in bed for an extra hour because you don't have anything planned.

Set a daily plan, make sure it's full and follow it. You'll find it's a great motivator. When the alarm clock goes off you'll think, "Boy, I've got to get up. I'm previewing 12 houses today, I've got two listing presentation appointments, and I've got to do three hours of prospecting. I'd better get started so I can get it all done." You're glad to see the morning! You're delighted because it's going to be another day for you to make money.

As you set out your daily plan, schedule a few minutes at the end of the day to make sure you're completing the tasks you set for yourself. If you're having difficulty in this area, you need to take a realistic look at how you are spending your time. You might be trying to do too much.

Remember, you'll need to allocate your time in relationship to your goals. If you only want to earn $9 per hour, you won't have to plan very much. Chances are you'll trip over that much business during the course of a year. However, if you want to earn $100 per hour, then you're going to have to plan for it. And don't be surprised if you exceed that figure. How you plan and spend your time will be a reflection of your goals.

Before you can be on your way to becoming a superstar, you may need to take some corrective action on some of the points I've named above. Don't be afraid to do it, because until you do, you may be spending a lot of time and earning a little money. Turn your time into supertime. In *Future Shock,* Alvin Toffler wrote, "The only thing that's constant is change," so get with it and change.

WEEKLY ACTIVITIES OF
THE SUPERSTAR

Okay, you've decided that you want to be a superstar and you know you have to make some changes in how you spend your time. But what do you really do with your time? What activities do superstars perform? They are, in a nutshell, only those activities that lead to the listing or selling of property.

You're going to love this first activity. Attend the weekly company sales meeting. "But Mike, they're so boring." Go anyway. Why? It's real simple. You'll find out about new sales listings. How else will you find out if you don't go? Maybe there's something special about the house, or maybe the seller is willing to help with the financing. Or (and you'll like this one) you may have the buyer of that house sitting in your files—and you wouldn't know if you didn't go to the meeting.

Also, ideas will be shared, and you just might learn something new. Maybe you have a problem for which you can get an answer; or you might hear of a problem you have not encountered and learn how to solve it. Wouldn't it be funny if that afternoon you encountered the same problem, only now, because you were at the meeting, you know its solution?

Another important reason for attending the company sales meetings is to show support for the system. That's important. Without the system, or the company, you would not have the opportunity to make money. Your presence at the meetings shows that you support the company and its programs. Besides, you may have a listing that needs to move quickly, and a co-worker might have the buyer sitting in his or her files. Whatever the reason, it's important for you to attend these meetings.

In addition to the company sales meetings, go on company caravans. Why? A couple of reasons. One, you continue to show support for the system; and two, you see the new office listings. Why is this important? One part of your listing presentation might be the number of agents in your office. "Mr. and Mrs. Seller, Banana Realty has 47 agents in our office, and they will all be working very hard to sell your house. We have an office caravan on Tuesday mornings, and all 47 agents will be here to see your house." Tuesday morning comes along and there are only seven agents on the caravan. Mr. and Mrs. Seller are wondering what happened to the other 40. As a result, your relationship and credibility with Mr. and Mrs. Seller have suffered. It's important that you go on the office caravans.

Also, this will give you an opportunity to preview houses before showing them to clients. Wouldn't it be a little embarrassing if one of your clients saw the great golden banana sign in front of a house, called you with some questions, and you weren't even aware that your office had listed the house? Wouldn't it be better if you were able to say, "Isn't that the white colonial with the rose garden in front?" Now you sound like you're a professional, and it's all due to taking the time to go on the office caravan.

Attend the Real Estate Board meetings. First of all, you'll meet agents that you'll later be involved with on a deal. In order to do this, however, you must sit with people you don't know and introduce yourself. "Hi. I'm Bill Smith from Banana Realty. What's your name?" That's not too difficult, and it will pay dividends when you later meet this person in a deal. Second, you'll hear about price reductions at the board meetings. "I've this house at 117 Elm Ave. Beautiful three-bedroom, two-bath ranch style. Jacuzzi in the back yard. The sellers just decided last night to reduce their asking price from $97,500 to $90,000." You're so excited. Sitting in your files is a buyer for a three-bedroom, two-bath ranch style with Jacuzzi who will pay $90,000. You can hardly wait to get to the phone!

Would you have found out about this price reduction if you had been back at the office or on the golf course? Oh sure, when the MLS book comes out next; but then so would all of the other agents. Even a $9 an hour agent can sell a house when he is given all of the right factors and stumbles in the right direction.

Remember, everything you do is directly related to the listing and selling of property. You're a superstar. You're worth $100 per hour and you show it, because you're no less a professional at what you do than a doctor, lawyer or accountant.

I have this dream of seeing all floor time abolished. That would really be exciting! I'm encouraged that a few brokerages are starting to move in this direction. Floor time is a complete waste of time for the superstar, so what are you going to do? Take advantage of it!

Making the Most of Floor Time

Having the floor carries with it some responsibilities that must be fulfilled. You must answer the phone and take legible and accurate messages. If your printing is more legible than your writing, print. The messages you take may be very important for someone's listing or sale, so don't screw them up. You certainly wouldn't want someone to make a mistake in taking a message for you, right? Show your fellow agents the same courtesy and respect.

In addition to the messages for other agents, you'll also receive sign and ad calls. Now, here's a chance to make some money. The phone rings.

"Banana Realty. Bill Smith. May I help you?"

"Yeah. I saw your ad for the three-bedroom, two-bath house on Royce St. I was just wondering how much it was."

"It's $192,000."

"Okay, thanks." (Click)

That's it, right? Nothing more you could do. You answered the question, what else could you do? That was your job, right? Wrong, wrong, wrong! Remember, your job is to list and sell property. Did you list any property? No. Did you sell any property? No. So you didn't do your job. Let's try it again.

> "Banana Realty. Bill Smith. May I help you?"
>
> "Yeah. I saw your ad for the three-bedroom, two-bath house on Royce St. I was just wondering how much it was."
>
> "It's in the $180,000 to $200,000 price range. Is that your price range?"
>
> "No. I didn't want to pay more than $130,000."
>
> "I have about a dozen homes in your price range that have three bedrooms and two baths. Would you like to see them now or at four o'clock this afternoon?"
>
> "My husband doesn't get home until three o'clock . . ."

Now you're doing your job. What you've done is turn a phone call into an appointment to show property, which, once you have qualified the buyer, could turn into a sale. Isn't that a great feeling? In case you're wondering, it does work!

Another way to take advantage of floor time is to do all of your paperwork during this period. Don't just sit at your desk with your feet propped up waiting for the phone to ring. Utilize this time to complete paperwork, prepare for the listing presentation you have that night, complete CMAs or work on your daily time planner. Whatever you decide to do, do something constructive rather than waiting for the phone to ring.

Stop and Smell the Roses

I've been telling you so far about the things that you should do if you're going to be a superstar, and I'm going to continue. You should take two days off a week. "But Mike. . . ." Don't "But Mike" me on this one. There's no discussion.

The burnout ratio in real estate is dramatically increased by the seven-day-a-week wonders. If you want to be around to be a superstar, you'll take two days off a week. You must realize that there's more to life than real estate. There is? Yes, Virginia, there is. "But Mike, what am I going to do with my days off? Besides, I need to earn the money."

I don't know what you're going to do with your days off, but I do have some suggestions. You can take a drive, go to a museum, take a hike, go to the beach, go to the mountains, window shop, go to the library, see a movie, read a book, etc. You'll notice that all of these have two things in common. One, they don't require much money, and two, they have little or nothing to do with real estate.

The idea is to refresh yourself and prepare for the coming week. It's a great idea and it works. Like everything I give you in this book, the idea of taking two days off is practical. You'll be sharper for your work week, you'll be better prepared mentally, you'll feel as though you have more control over your destiny, and you'll feel like a super-star. Believe me, once you begin to feel like a superstar, you'll begin to act like one.

To help you enjoy your days off, get rid of your beepers and car phones. Also, take your home phone number off your business card. No emergency could happen at the office that would require them to reach you. If a client wants you, just leave instructions with the office to offer assistance until you return. But if you've delegated work to the professionals, chances are they won't need you. The benefits of taking two days off outweigh the drawbacks.

The No-Show Factor

If you don't show property, you can't sell property. That's really basic. There aren't too many people in this world who would buy a house sight unseen, so you've got to show clients property if you're going to be a superstar.

What is the biggest problem when it comes to showing clients property? It's the no-show factor, right? We've all had no-shows, even superstars—but superstars keep no-shows to a minimum. How? By calling to make appointments to show property early in the week.

What day is best for calling for appointments? Tuesdays seem to be best. On Monday you're probably putting together the paperwork to send to your escrow officer for the three houses you sold on the weekend, so that may be a little hectic. Also, you're taking the time to plan the rest of your week. Mondays also may be hectic for working clients.

The reason for calling a client on Tuesday to make an appointment to show houses is quite simple. You get to them before another agent has the opportunity. Do you really think these clients are working with you exclusively? Remember CU? The second course instructs clients to get as many real estate agents working for them as possible. Why? Because it doesn't cost them a penny. Remember, you don't get paid until there's a sale, and clients are as aware of this as you are.

Also, by calling on Tuesday you can, and should, immediately send them a confirming note. If you called later in the week, a confirming note would arrive too late to be effective. Then, on the day before the appointment, call the client and reconfirm the time of the appointment.

What's going to happen to another agent who calls later in the week, like about Thursday, to make an appointment with these clients? Mr. and Mrs. Client will say they already have an appointment to see property. Following these steps will cut down on the client no-show factor.

Remember, now that you're thinking like a superstar, you're delegating tasks out to professionals, right? This is where delegation will pay off. Take a day early in the week, like Tuesday or Wednesday, to follow up on all of your transactions in process. Instead of making four different calls to four different escrow officers or mortgage bankers, you'll be making one call to each professional.

Think of the time you'll save! It's going to be great. Instead of making eight, 12 or 16 calls, you're only making two, three or four calls. The calls are not only fewer in number, they will be shorter in duration. Instead of hearing about problems, you'll be hearing about solutions. Then you can report to your clients that all is progressing as it should. What will this leave more time for? That's right, listing and selling. Now you're beginning to act as if your time is worth $100 per hour. You're acting like a superstar!

The Importance of Regular Contact

Do you know what the biggest complaint of sellers is regarding the listing agent? I'll tell you. "I never heard from the agent after we listed our house." Now, does that make any sense? You worked hard to get that listing. Yes, it might be a little overpriced, or there wasn't much activity during the past week regarding that house; but superstars stay in weekly contact with their sellers. There really isn't any alternative.

Why? Because Mr. and Mrs. Seller have friends who may want to sell their houses, so if you have done a good job for them, they will refer their friends to you. That word "refer" is a golden word for the superstar. It makes the listing presentation so much easier, because you have already been established in the seller's mind as a professional.

What happens if you have nothing to report when you call your sellers? If the house is overpriced, you can use the call to get them to lower the price.

"Mr. [or Mrs.] Seller, there hasn't been any activity on your house this week. Yes, I know that the two houses down the street sold this week, but they were asking $7,500 less than you are. Would you consider lowering the price so I can sell your house, too?" Chances are they will say yes, if they really want to move.

Remember, whether you have a full report of activity to give the sellers or you want them to lower the price, call them weekly. You'll maintain your relationship with them and further establish yourself as a professional.

Take a Break!

Schedule time for lunch. Sounds too obvious, doesn't it? However, real estate sales agents rarely admit to eating lunch. They're kind of closet eaters, in that they continually nibble in the office all day long. And what they eat usually falls into the general category of junk food.

If you're going to act like a superstar, look like a superstar. Schedule an hour out of each day prior to 4 P.M. to eat lunch. There are two reasons for this. First, if you take one hour away from real estate during the middle of the day, you'll maintain your sanity. You need this time to yourself unless you want to come across as a crazy person who has no control of his or her life.

The second reason is physical health. Do you want to lose a little weight? Then eat 70 percent of your food prior to 4 P.M. Unfortunately, real estate sales agents have a tendency to eat a large, late lunch, followed by a large, late dinner. Dinner is immediately followed by going to bed. What do you think happens to all the calories you took in at dinner? Well, unless you exercise in your sleep, they turn to fat. So, don't only act like a superstar, look like one; eat most of your food prior to 4 P.M.

The Early Bird Gets Richer

The time you spend in the office working on follow-ups should be divided into two 30-minute blocks: one early in the morning and one in the later afternoon. Use your time productively and get your work done.

When I was selling real estate, I went into the office at 7 A.M. and at 5 or 6 P.M. Why those times? Most real estate agents never get to the office before 9 A.M., so I had the office to myself before they got there. In fact, I was in and out before most of my fellow agents arrived in the morning. The same thought applies to the later afternoon times; most agents had already left for home by the time I arrived.

Do you remember who some of the biggest time thieves are next to clients? Yes, your fellow agents. Good ol' Fred and Mary, who want to talk to you about their problems. But guess what? If you aren't there, they can't talk to you, so your time will be more productive. Also, the phone rarely rings at 7 A.M., so you can work undisturbed.

"But Mike, I care about my fellow agents." If you care that much about them, go to school and become a psychologist so you can charge them while you listen. Right now, they're taking money out of your pocket by talking to you. You're in real estate to make money, right? So, make money by being productive. It's not productive to be in the office listening to the problems of your fellow agents. If you're listening to them, you can't get your work done. End of argument.

Get Out and Scout!

You must see property daily. Anybody who is not seeing property daily is not in the real estate business—and certainly is not on the way to becoming a superstar. It's important. Why?

You'll become a better listing agent by knowing what is on the market. You'll know what kind of house is selling for how much. Doesn't it make sense to see property in the neighborhood of a house where you have a listing presentation that night? Yes, it does. Plus, more knowledge makes you a stronger agent, and a stronger agent is closer to becoming a superstar and that SIX-figure income.

If you're out seeing property daily, you'll find all of the FSBOs. Don't be afraid to stop and talk to them. Ask them why they're going FSBO. They can be a rich source of listings, so cultivate them. Remember, there are only two responsibilities of the real estate sales agent. What are they? To list and sell property. You can't list 'em if you don't talk to 'em.

As you're out seeing property, you're bound to come across listings that are about to expire for one reason or another. The sellers may not be happy with their current real estate agent, so take advantage of the situation and make an appointment to see them when the listing expires.

Think of the market knowledge you'll build if you're out seeing property daily. That knowledge will assist you when a client wants to know if a certain kind of house is available. You're building an inventory for your buyers so that you'll know the answer when they have a question. This kind of knowledge does not come from the MLS, it comes from the hands-on experience that only seeing property daily can give you.

This same knowledge will aid you when you want to switch an ad call to a house that better suits their needs. You'll know what is available to them and, in turn, you'll become the professional they will learn to depend upon. Now you're becoming a superstar. Now, instead of just *thinking* SIX, you're *achieving* SIX.

If you're seeing houses every day, you'll be talking to buyers every day. "But Mike, I thought you said I'm supposed to see property that is for sale every day." That's right, but in talking to sellers, you're in fact talking to buyers. What?

Studies show that 50 percent of the sellers are going to buy a house in the same area. In a lot of cases, the listing agent hasn't had the courage to ask the seller to look at property because he hasn't sold their house. The listing agent might not feel as though he has done his job until the house has sold, and fear keeps him from asking the sellers to look at other properties. Don't be afraid to ask. Start working with those clients now to help them find a house, and in the meantime you might be able to find a buyer for their current house. A double commission can be quite a motivating factor!

Do you see why it's so important to see property daily? It makes you a stronger agent, and by being a stronger agent you become a better agent. Superstars are better agents. And wealthier agents!

Prospecting is important to schedule and do. Where else are you going to get clients, if not from prospecting? For now, schedule it into your weekly plan on a daily basis; there will be more information on it later.

There's Always Room for (Self-) Improvement

If you don't grow personally, you shrink and shrivel. Who wants to buy real estate from a prune? Quite simply, nobody. This is why it's important to schedule into your weekly plan a time for education and physical improvement.

If you're not presented with new mental challenges on a regular basis, you'll stagnate. There are no ifs, ands or buts about it. You have to expand your mind if you're to be a well-rounded person. I've included a reading list that you may want to use as a starting place to increase your storehouse of knowledge. Another place to begin might be your local community college. These colleges offer courses that cover a wide variety of subjects at a reasonable cost.

Physical improvement time is as important as education time, and it should be scheduled for 30 minutes five times a week. No, you can't schedule it for two and one-half hours on your days off. You need to exercise on at least three different days. There's a direct correlation between physical condition and production. How are you going to run the race if you can't even get in it?

There will be those times when, because of sheer persistence, you're able to make a sale or get a listing. You simply have to outlast the buyer, seller or other agent. If you can't last longer than the buyer, seller or other agent, how are you going to make the SIX-figure income? You're not. This is where physical conditioning will play a very important part of your success in achieving superstardom.

And finally, there is planning time. Yes, you must schedule planning time. You must spend at least 30 minutes a week organizing your time. In the beginning, you'll be spending more than 30 minutes. However, as you become more experienced, you'll find that the amount of time you have to devote to planning shrinks.

Also, in order to be most effective, plan out as far in advance as possible. Your goal should be to have the next six months planned. Six months? "But Mike, I like spontaneity in my life." Great! Be spontaneous and be poor. If you'll plan out the next six months, you'll find it easier to become a superstar. Remember, a full daily planner can help motivate you to success.

A wise person once said: "Time, you should be its master, and not let it master you. You cannot master yourself unless you master your time."

MIKE FERRY'S READING LIST

Now, I'm not advocating that you rush right out to the bookstore and buy these books. Most, if not all of them, will be available at the public library.

1. *Fit or Fat* by Covert Bailey
2. *Further Up the Organization* by Robert Townsend
3. *Future Shock* by Alvin Toffler
4. *Hour Power* by John Lee
5. *How I Raised Myself from Failure to Success in Selling* by Frank Bettger
6. *How To List and Sell Real Estate,* 2nd ed., by Danielle Kennedy
7. *How To Win Friends and Influence People,* Rev. Ed., by Dale Carnegie and Dorothy Carnegie
8. *Iacocca: An Autobiography* by Lee Iacocca and William Novak
9. *Inner Game of Tennis* by W. Timothy Gallowey
10. *In Search of Excellence: Lessons from America's Best Run Companies* by Thomas J. Peters and Robert H. Waterman
11. *Man's Search for Meaning* by Victor E. Frankl
12. *Megatrends* by John Naisbitt
13. *Motivation and the Personality* by Abraham Maslow
14. *Real Estate People* by Robert Shook
15. *Reality Therapy: A New Approach to Psychiatry* by William Glasser
16. *Schools Without Failures* by William Glasser
17. *Stress Without Distress* by Hans Selye
18. *The Art of Japanese Management* by Richard T. Pascale and Anthony G. Athos
19. *The Complete Book of Running* by James F. Fixx
20. *The Magic of Thinking Big* by David J. Schwartz
21. *The One Minute Manager* by Kenneth Blanchard and Spencer Johnson
22. *The One Minute Salesperson* by Spencer Johnson and Larry Wilson
23. *The Peter Principle* by Laurence J. Peter and Raymond Hull
24. *The Prodigal Daughter* by Jeffery Archer
25. *The Stress of Life,* 2nd ed., by Hans Selye
26. *The Third Wave* by Alvin Toffler

27. *Think and Grow Rich* by Napoleon Hill
28. *This Is Earl Nightingale* by Earl Nightingale
29. *Thrive on Stress: How To Make It Work for You* by Richard Sharpe
30. *Tough Times Don't Last—Tough People Do* by Robert H. Schuller
31. *What They Don't Teach You at the Harvard Business School* by Mark H. McCormack
32. *You Are Not the Target* by Laura A. Huxley
33. *Your Erroneous Zones* by Wayne W. Dyer

HOW TO FILL OUT A WEEKLY PLANNER

I've given you a lot of items to put in your weekly planner. Do you know why? It's very simple: There's a lot to do if you're going to be a superstar.

Why do you think that only 2 percent of real estate agents make in excess of $75,000? Is it because of a lack of business? No! Is it because they don't want to make $75,000? No! Why? It's because the average agent, the $9 per hour agent, doesn't know what to do to make SIX figures.

The average real estate agent is going to spend 40 to 50 marginally productive hours a week at the real estate business. By organizing a weekly planner, you'll be spending the same amount of time working, but you'll be more productive. The more productive you are, the more money you'll make. It's just that simple.

A basic rule about filling out a weekly planner: USE A PENCIL. Why? Because your plans might change, and it's easier and less confusing to erase a pencil mark than to scratch out ink.

The question you must ask at this point is, "How much time should I allow for the things I need to do on a weekly basis?" I'm going to tell you right now, and you'll be surprised at how much time you really have in a week to make money:

- *Sales meeting*—Just use an average length of time.
- *Company caravan*—This normally follows the sales meeting.
- *Real estate board meeting*—Just schedule it in.

- *Two days off*—Pick 'em and make it in big letters. These are full days off, not two half-days.
- *Calls for showing appointments*—Monday or Tuesday between 6 and 8 P.M. Just block out one hour.
- *Follow-up on closings*—One hour on either Tuesday or Wednesday morning or late afternoon.
- *Follow-up on listings*—One hour later in the week, Thursday or Friday, late afternoon or early evening to call your sellers.
- *Lunch*—One hour on each day that you work.
- *Office time*—Thirty minutes early in the morning and late in the afternoon on each day that you work. Don't schedule it later than 9:30 in the morning. Why? Because that's when all of the other agents will arrive, and you won't be able to get anything done.
- *Previewing property*—Two-hour segments three times a week to see other brokers' listings. I suggest that you do this during the day.
- *Physical improvement*—Thirty minutes five times a week.
- *Prospecting*—A total of ten hours in one-hour block minimums. Yes, you can do it in three-hour blocks.

Now, after you've filled out the weekly planner, add up the number of hours you're actually working. This excludes the hour for lunch and the thirty minutes for physical improvement. You'll be surprised! The total for the week should be between 28 and 32 hours. This allows plenty of time for the listing and showing of property. You could begin to make some real money. You could begin to not only *think* SIX, but *make* SIX. Now you've started to create your own supertime.

You can become a superstar. It may mean that you have to add some discipline to your life, but the rewards of that discipline far outweigh the price. Becoming a superstar means that you'll be investing time in yourself and your profession in order to become one of the best real estate sales agents in the country, and the best in your office. Are you ready to make that investment of time?

"No matter what we want personally, we have to pay the price with our time."

I've shown you how to use your time; the results are up to you. Do it!

Hi Mike,

During the past five years you've helped me in more ways than you knew. First and foremost, I admit it took me a number of months to implement all the ideas that you shared in the Action Workshop. Boy, do they work! I guess the biggest advantage I've had, and I knew this as I sat in the room with you during various programs, is that most people believe if they try the things you suggest, their real estate careers can skyrocket like mine has.

All you asked us to do was to prospect every day, learn our presentations, then go out and do it. It's incredible how simple it is, how well it works and how much money you make when you do it.

I guess I've always been considered strong in my approach, and all I ever really needed was somebody to put me on the right track for prospecting, so I could use all of my energy to create more listings and sales.

You've been telling people for the last two or three years that I'm the number-one agent in North America. I'm not sure if I am or not, but my goal in 1992 is 300 transactions, and it's all because you not only taught me but *forced* me to prospect. Thanks.

Walter S.

CHAPTER 3

Superstar Prospecting Techniques

Now that you have a time management system, it's important for you to know what to do during the time allocated for certain activities. Remember, all of your activities have a common goal. What is it? That's right! To obtain a listing or a sale.

Prospecting is the backbone of your business. Prospecting is what will ultimately lead to that listing or sale. Prospecting, or your lack of it, will determine whether you're really a $100 per hour real estate sales agent or one of those $9 per hour real estate people.

This chapter covers the following topics:

- The Importance of Prospecting
- High and Low Impact Prospecting
- The Qualities of Great Prospectors
- Methods of Prospecting

Pay attention to what you read and follow instructions, and you'll actually become worth $100 per hour, instead of just thinking that you are. But in order to earn that SIX-figure income, the first thing you must do is imagine yourself earning it, then go out and do it.

THE IMPORTANCE OF PROSPECTING

How important is prospecting? Well, just how important is it that you breathe? Drink water? Eat? Do you begin to get the idea that prospecting is important, even essential, to your success in real estate? It is.

Since you're involved in just two types of transactions, listing and selling, and both of those need people to instigate and complete them, it follows that if you find the people who have a need to buy or sell real estate, you'll be successful. "But, Mike, how am I going to find those people?" By prospecting.

"But, Mike, that's hard work." There's no doubt about that. However, do you think there's any broker around who's going to pay you $100 per hour just to grace the office? No, there isn't. Even the $10 per hour folks have to close a deal now and then just to be able to come into the office and drink coffee in the morning. Sure, prospecting is hard work, but do you want to receive $10 per hour or $100 per hour? That's a pretty easy decision for most of you.

I think that I better let you in on a little secret right now, and this is just for the $100 per hour folks. All of you $10 real estate people just skip a paragraph, we'll catch up with you. That won't present too much of a problem, since $100 sales agents have to move about 11 times better (not faster) than the $10 people.

Now, to the secret. Listen, be thankful for the $10 per hour folks. Why? Because they make it so much easier for you. Yes, that's true. I know that there are a lot of those folks out there, but it cuts down on the competition. How? Because they will never do anything that I suggest—or, if they do, they only give it about a 10 percent effort. So, if they're occupying a desk instead of another $100 per hour real estate sales agent, be thankful. In fact, you may want to initiate a "Slug Appreciation Day" or "Agent Appreciation Day." Don't worry, if you follow my advice, you'll be able to afford it. You see, it would actually be tougher for you to be that $100 sales agent if there were a lot of them (like about 30,000). But since there aren't, and probably won't be, you don't have any worries.

Now, we should all be back together. Prospecting for precious metals and gems has been going on for centuries in all parts of the world. You're literally doing the same thing. Prospectors were looking for valuables that, when found, would be turned into money. Listings and sales, when found, are money. They were looking for gold, silver and diamonds. You're looking for people who want to buy or sell real property.

Not only do the real estate sales agent and the prospector have the goal of earning money from their findings in common, they both work very hard to do so. Prospectors, if successful, know everything about whatever they are looking for and dedicate themselves to that search. Successful real estate sales agents dedicate themselves equally in their prospecting for listings and sales.

There's a word that you must learn if you're to be a successful real estate sales agent. A little hint: It's a four-letter word beginning with the letter F. Got it? No, not that word. The word is *fine*. What a great all-around response for anything that might be said to you as you're prospecting!

Take my word for it; you'll be using *fine* quite often as you respond to people while prospecting. Why? Well, first of all, *fine* can be used as a positive response or a neutral response. For example, say that you've just knocked on a cold door (more about those later), and the person who answers the door asks you to list their house. Now, you've got a couple of choices. You could faint from shock, scream with delight, tell them to wait until you can go through a listing presentation or say "Fine," and make the listing appointment.

Take another kind of case. You knock on the door and the person who answers is very, very negative about real estate sales agents. This person has categorized real estate sales agents just above chronic halitosis but below offensive body odor. Get the picture? Instead of telling him what you think of his manners or taking personal offense at his remarks, say "Fine," thank him for his time and go on to the next door. *Fine* can indeed keep you out of trouble. Take just a moment to practice saying *Fine,* and be careful of voice inflection. It's not *FINE!* It's a bit more calm; an in-control inflection or tone. Try putting a smile on your face as you say it. That's better. It doesn't hurt to practice this every once in awhile, okay? Fine.

HIGH- AND LOW-IMPACT PROSPECTING

There are two kinds of prospecting: high-impact and low-impact. It might be more descriptive if you were to think of them as high-income and low-income prospecting. That kind of description will at least give you an idea of their relative merits.

If you're a $10 per hour real estate person, then you're probably involved in low-impact prospecting. "But Mike, I'm not involved in prospecting at all." Exactly my point. Low-impact prospecting is dependent upon the client coming to you. Now, not being stupid, you understand the necessity of remaining in a fixed location like your office, so you're easier to find. Makes sense to me.

Low-impact prospectors are dependent upon sign and ad calls, walk-ins and the rare person who wants to buy the open house at which the prospector is presiding. It's self-limiting; however, you can make a living at it that's worth about $10 per hour.

When I was studying for the real estate exam, I went around to various real estate offices to find out where I might like to work once I received my license. One afternoon I went into an office that was owned by a large company that's no longer in business. (You'll see why in a moment.) The manager did not have time to see me, so he turned me over to one of his "star salesmen." The only thing I remember from our discussion was this "salesman" telling me that I would never have to prospect, because I could make a "good living" from the ad calls. Now, can you understand why this company is no longer in business? A whole company based on low-impact prospecting! Unbelievable!

On the other hand, there's high-impact prospecting. Thank heavens! Without high-impact prospecting, those real estate people who wait for the ad calls would never make a dime. You see, high-impact prospecting means going out to where the people are, to where business is to be found. High-impact prospectors go out and list the houses so that the low-impact folks can stay in the office and take sales orders. And we all know how often that happens. It would be appropriate for the low-income people to have a "High-Impact Appreciation Day," but they can't afford it.

Yes, you read that correctly. You go out to find business instead of waiting for it to find you. High-impact prospecting means that you'll be talking to a lot of people daily. You can no longer be a secret real estate agent. You have to become a "known" agent. Why? Because you won't be in the office to take the orders—you'll be out of the office looking for the business. And if someone should want to walk up and list his or her house, that person has to know that you're a real estate sales professional. That does make sense, doesn't it?

You must remember that real estate, like most sales professions, is a numbers game. What does this mean? It means that when you talk to so many people, you can expect to make a deal. In real estate, averages show that you'll need to talk to 100 people to get one listing or sale. Can you understand why you aren't going to make it by talking with 23 people a day? At that rate, you would get a deal every five weeks—that's ten deals a year. That's right on target for the $10 per hour crew!

Is there any reason you can't have ten deals per month? There really isn't. It will just take talking to a lot of people and not being a secret real estate agent.

A couple of years ago, I was leading an Action Workshop in the San Fernando Valley of Southern California. Before I go on, let me tell you that the Valley is one of the most competitive markets in America. It seems to a lot of agents that the Valley has been farmed and prospected to death—at least to the point where the owners and sellers may have spoken to more real estate people than you may ever meet.

Mary, who had been in the business for about three months, completed a homework assignment that I had given the group on prospecting. The assignment was to talk to 100 people a day about listing or selling property. Mary talked to 510 people during that week. She was new; she didn't know any better. What did she get for her efforts? FIVE, count 'em, FIVE signed listing contracts in the course of one week. Not too shabby! In addition, she had six other appointments the next week to give her listing presentation.

Now, in case you have a difficult time figuring it out, Mary got 11 appointments and five listings in the course of one week. That's more than some of you will get in six months. Now, if she were to just stay at that pace, Mary would make 250 deals in one year. Mary is definitely a superstar. She is doing more than thinking SIX, she is doing SIX. How did she do it? Mary followed instructions, that's all. Believe me, there aren't many of you who live and work in the kind of area that Mary had to work in, so please don't say, "But Mike, my area is different." My response would be, "Yes, it's different . . . it's easier!" Get the picture?

Remember that the more people you talk to, the more people you'll make deals with and the more money you'll make. Right? So follow instructions. The worst thing that can be said to you by a prospect, who is by definition a stranger, is "No." You'll have to hear about 99 *no*'s to get one *yes*. Get used to the idea. Count the *no*'s, because as you get closer to the 99th *no*, you're getting closer to that wonderful *yes*. This is high-impact prospecting. This is high-income prospecting. This is superstar prospecting!

Just so you understand: Farming is not true prospecting. Farming is a method, but it should not be your only method. I can only hope that farming will one day be discontinued in real estate, because it's generally a great waste of time. "But Mike, I got five deals out of my farm last year." Great—but in the same time that it took you to get those five deals, you could have had 25 or 50 deals if you were using other methods of prospecting. More about farming later.

QUALITIES OF GREAT PROSPECTORS

All of the great prospectors, all of the superstars, all of the people who are *doing* SIX instead of just *thinking* SIX have some qualities in common. Doesn't it make sense that you would want to adopt these same qualities as your own if you're going to be successful in real estate? Of course it does! The question really is, why try to blaze a new trail when there's one clearly marked for you to follow? That would mean increased work, and you're going to be busy enough if you're going to be making SIX.

Absence

What qualities do all great prospectors share? Among others, great prospectors stay out of the office. My first day in real estate made that pretty clear to me. I arrived at the office at 9 A.M. excited and ready to make those deals. My manager welcomed me to the office, showed me where my desk and telephone were, and told me to sit down. After sitting down, I asked him what I should do. He responded that I should watch the other agents. I did so. For three boring hours I watched real estate agents sitting around the office. Nobody was making any deals.

I was beginning to go nuts and thought that this was definitely not what I had in mind.

At the end of three hours, the manager came back out to me and asked if I was ready to work. When I said yes, he told me to go out of the office. Once we were outside, he said to go back into the office. We repeated this about three times until I asked, "What are we doing?"

He said that we were practicing leaving the office. It was obvious to me that the other agents needed to practice the same thing, but being new, I kept my mouth shut. He told me that most agents did not know how to leave the office, and he just wanted to make sure that I knew how.

We then practiced getting in and out of my car (I got the idea pretty fast on this one). He then proceeded to explain to me the function of the two pedals that were located on the floor of the driver's side of the car. "The right one makes you go forward; the left one makes you stop. Don't be afraid to use the left pedal."

What was he doing? He was telling me that if I wanted to be successful in real estate, I should stay out of the office. That's what I'm telling you: STAY OUT OF THE OFFICE! You will not find prospects by sitting around your office. What will you find? That's right—other agents.

Attentiveness

If you want to be a great prospector, you must become a great listener. We have a tendency to worry more about what we are going to say next than what our prospect is saying. What will help to cure us of this momentary deafness? Trigger cards.

Trigger cards are nothing more or less than 5"x 8" index cards with questions written on them. Not notes on what to say when you get a specific objection, but specific questions that will assist you in determining if the prospect currently needs your services or might need them in the future. Don't be bashful about referring to the cards; nobody is born an expert at prospecting. It only comes with practice. Some of the experts, the superstars, continue to use trigger cards so they won't forget an important question.

"But Mike, using trigger cards seems so unprofessional." Does it? Would you want a surgeon to operate on you without benefit of x-rays? What are x-rays, if not a glorified trigger card? And surgeons constantly refer to them during the course of an operation. Now, if a surgeon needs trigger cards (x-rays), don't you think that you might need them as well? I know that I would not want my doctor, no matter how many times he has performed the surgery, to open me without x-rays first. Do you really want to talk to a prospect without benefit of trigger cards? No, I didn't think so. Remember, the trigger cards are there to help you listen to what the prospect is saying.

After I had been in the business awhile, my neighbors in Huntington Beach, Calif., told me that they wanted to sell their homes and asked me if I would list them for sale. This wasn't just one neighbor, this was one on each side of my house. Remember, I was out each day talking to 100 people about listing or selling property, and here were two "freebies" just waiting for me to sit down and list their property. All I had to do was *hear* that they wanted to list. But. . . .

I came home about two weeks later and saw that both homes had a competing company's signs in their front yards. I was fit to be tied. I went up to one of them and asked, "Why didn't you list with me?" His response: "I tried to, but you didn't listen to me." That little lesson cost me two commissions. I was not able to sell their old houses, but I was able to sell them their new houses. Please learn from my mistake.

Awareness

Great prospectors are aware of what is going on around them. I certainly became aware of what was going on around me when I saw the competing company's signs on my neighbor's lawns! You must be alert to those around you; you must always have your antennae out, looking for those people who want to buy or sell real estate. You know what the amazing thing is? They're all around you. You literally cannot escape from people who want to buy or sell real estate, even if you wanted to!

Do you remember the gas lines of the late seventies? I certainly do. One day I got in a line—a long line—to purchase some gas. Admittedly, I'm not a very patient person when it comes to waiting. After about two hours it was my turn; I was finally at the head of the line. An attendant approached me with a smile and asked how much gas I wanted. I clenched my teeth and said, "Fill it up. Where is the owner of this station?" The kid pointed to a man sitting near the station office and then hurried to fill my car with gas. I walked over to the man who was sitting there and asked him, without benefit of introduction, "Do you want to buy or sell real estate?" What was his reply? "I couldn't possibly do it before this Friday." Guess where I was Friday evening. That's right—I was listing his house. Not only did I list his house, I sold it and sold him another house. I received three commission checks because I was not afraid to tell people that I was a real estate sales agent.

There are always buyers and sellers of real estate. Wherever you go you can find them. You just have to be aware that they're out there, and ask if you can help them.

Follow-Up

Great prospectors follow up on their leads immediately. Not after the football game, not after a walk, immediately. Why? Because the longer you wait, the harder it is to follow up. The harder it becomes to make that call. Phone messages keep piling up on your desk, waiting to be returned. Then you commit one of the biggest sins of all; you don't return the calls. "But Mike, I don't have time to return all of my calls." Make the time. Even if it's just to say that you can't talk right then, but you'll get back to them tomorrow. Of course, you have to get back to them the next day, but at least you're not ignoring them. Don't let this slide!

How often should you be calling your buyer and seller leads? Every day. Once again, you should be calling your buyer and seller leads daily. Why? Because it helps to establish the relationship and assists you in gaining control. "But Mike, what am I going to say?" It's very simple. "Mr. Buyer, I just wanted to let you know that I'm still looking for your house." Or, "Mrs. Seller, I just wanted to let you know that I just listed another house in your area." Get the idea? Keep it short and to the point. Buyer and seller prospects are busy people, too.

One more thing. Make all of your calls early in the morning. By early, I mean between 7 and 8 A.M. Yes, people are up that early, and they will begin to expect you to call during that time. So call them. This is especially effective if you have told them during a presentation that you'll call them at a specific time, so why not make it early in the morning?

Resilience

Great prospectors know how to handle rejection. Rejection comes from two basic sources: people you know, and people you don't know. You have to learn when to take the rejection personally and when to let it roll off your back.

When rejection comes from a close friend or loved one, take it personally. This kind of rejection is not for a group at large. It's meant for you, so take it that way. And if you're lucky, you'll learn from it. However, as a real estate sales agent who's thinking SIX, you won't be receiving that much of this kind of rejection.

So what kind of rejection will you be receiving? The kind that's aimed at large groups of people, which, because of its very nature, you should not take to heart. This is like mud thrown at a wall. The difference is that you have the choice as to whether or not it will stick to you. Don't let it stick!

What makes a prospect react that way to you? First, you must realize that he is not reacting to you specifically. He is responding to some negative experience he has had with a real estate person. Remember, most people who are in the real estate business are not professionals, so it's more likely than not that a prospect has had a negative real estate experience. You have to put those reactions behind you and realize that you're a professional—every bit as professional as an accountant, lawyer or doctor. You're as capable in your field as they are in theirs. You're a professional at listing and selling property.

There's a cliche in sales: "Every *no* brings you that much closer to a *yes*." It may sound a little trite, but it's true. Remember, you can expect one deal for every 100 contacts. What does that tell you? You need 99 *no*'s to get one *yes*. So love those *no*'s. If you're not busy, if you're not thinking SIX, if you're not on your way to becoming a superstar, then you're not going to get a lot of *no*'s. You're also not going to be making any money. So, go for the *no*'s.

"No" is the worst that a prospect can tell you. Will that hurt you? No, it won't. Here's an idea; why not have a office contest collecting *no*'s? The one with the most no's wins. Managers, if you're reading this, pay attention, because this is a pretty good idea.

When is the best time to prospect, to collect those no's? Something can be wrong with any time you can think of: Early morning is breakfast time; mid-morning you don't want to disturb anybody cleaning house;

noon is your lunchtime; mid-afternoon there's little league, football or soccer; early evening is dinnertime; and, late evening is bedtime. Sounds a little discouraging, doesn't it? You know, I didn't make up those objections; all of them came out of a seminar in Phoenix a few years ago. Phoenix might not be such a bad place to work if that's the prevalent attitude toward prospecting.

So when is the best time to prospect? Any time. Whenever you want. From early morning to late evening, there's no best time. For a superstar, prospecting can be done at any time and any place. Let the $10 per hour person figure out why he or she can't prospect; the $100 per hour sales agent will prospect whenever opportunity knocks.

Do you know what is as hard for some agents to deal with as rejection? Acceptance. Can you believe that? They condition themselves to hearing "no" so much that when they finally get a "yes," they don't know what to do. Get used to the idea that sooner or later you're bound to hear someone say, "List my house," so be ready for it when it happens. Accept it as part of what is due you for your efforts.

Let's take another look at the numbers. For every 100 people that you talk to, you should get one deal. What does that mean in terms of money? You know, those green pieces of paper with dead presidents' pictures on the front? Assuming a selling price of, say, $100,000, your basic commission of 6 percent with broker's split would mean $1,500 coming to you, right? Right.

Now, you've talked to 100 people to get that deal. Each person who told you "no" put you that much closer to a "yes," right? Right. Stay with me, now. If $1,500 divided by 100 people equals $15 per person, then each *no* was worth $15. So the next time you get a *no* when you're out prospecting, thank the person who said it.

Creativity

The great prospectors have learned to become more creative. This is what keeps it from becoming boring and makes it fun. "But Mike, how can prospecting be fun?" By adding a little creativity and a little individuality. Creativity is nothing more than rearranging old things in a new way, or finding a new way.

Have you ever had a boring day in real estate? Sure you have. Why? Because you were doing the same old thing in the same old way. That approach makes whatever you're doing as boring as stale bread. What's the answer? Change the way you're doing things.

I was out prospecting one day. I had knocked on three cold doors and had been rejected by all three. Each time, I told the prospect, "Fine, thank you for your time," and moved on to the next door. Well, after three rejections I was ready to do anything but more prospecting. The beach was looking real good. So was the golf course. Even the idea of sitting in an empty bowling alley seemed appealing. I knew that none of those presented a realistic alternative to what I was doing, so I took a minute to sit in my car and think.

Then it hit me. I'd take a survey and find out how to keep my company's name and my name in front of these people without ever having to prospect again. Now, that sounded real good to me. The first two doors were answered by women who told me in no uncertain terms what they thought of real estate people and companies. I began to think that this was not such a hot idea, but I kept on going. After 30 doors, I got a listing appointment for that night.

Why did I get that listing appointment? Because I tried something new. It wasn't the same old approach that people were used to hearing. I tried some originality. I used creativity. And remember, when you try something new, give it a chance. Be persistent. Don't give up just because one prospect has a bad opinion of real estate people, or some $10 per hour agent tells you that it won't work. Ignore them and go forward. Going backward leads to poverty. Forward is where the money is to be found.

METHODS OF PROSPECTING

"Okay, Mike, those are the qualities that great prospectors have; but how about telling *me* how to prospect?" I'm right there, right now. It's great to know that you're excited about learning how to prospect.

One of the most important things to learn is that you should use more than one method of prospecting. In fact, you should use five or six different methods. Why? So you won't become dependent on one method that may not give you the best results—like farming. Also, if you're using five or six methods on a regular basis, you won't become bored with any one method. You'll literally have a different method for each day of the week.

One more item. How often should you prospect? Every day. If you're going to become a superstar, and if you intend to think SIX, then you really don't have a choice.

A few more words about high-impact and low-impact prospecting. Almost all of the methods I'm going to give you can be used as either high- or low-impact prospecting. Do you remember the difference? Do the words high income and low income sound familiar? This is where you get to decide if you're worth $10 or $100 per hour.

If you're willing to talk to 100 people a day, then you're worth $100 per hour. You're on your way to becoming a superstar. You're on your way to the SIX-figure income.

However, if you decide that you're only worth $10 per hour, then you don't need to talk to very many people a day. Maybe just five or six people will do. You'll probably trip over enough business in the course of a year to make $10 per hour. (I have a question for you $10 folks: Why don't you go to work for the government? You'd earn more, have a pension and have health insurance. Plus, because you aren't involved in that many deals, you'd screw things up less for the superstars. It's just an idea.)

Why don't people prospect more? Is it because they're afraid of rejection, afraid of the prospects, or because they don't know what to say? Do you notice that I did not include "not enough time"? We both know that you have the time, because you're using a time management system now, right?

If not knowing what to say was your reason for not prospecting, get ready to toss that excuse out the window. How can you know and remember what to say to a prospect? By writing it out. Yes, have it scripted. When the lawyer talks to a witness or the jury, he or she has notes; the doctor has x-rays; the superstar has trigger cards. You can even make your own. If you choose to do that, use 5" × 8" index cards, print clearly and use at least two different colors of ink, so it's easy for you to follow without getting lost.

"But Mike, that seems so Mickey Mouse. Besides, I never forget anything when I'm talking to a client." Well, number one, do you have any idea how much good ol' Mickey Mouse is worth today? A lot. That's a lot followed by a bunch of zeroes. Number two, you mean to say that you've never forgotten a client's name? That you've never said the wrong thing at the wrong time? These trigger cards prevent you from saying the wrong thing or from forgetting what to say. Why? Because you'll always have the right thing to say in front of you.

Believe me, trigger cards will help you. They will give you confidence and your prospecting will go faster. You'll be more professional, because you won't be stumbling over your own tongue for something to say. As a result of being more professional, of knowing what to say and being quick and decisive, you'll win the prospect's confidence and become his or her real estate professional. And what will happen when you become the prospect's real estate professional? You'll be making more trips to the bank to deposit those commission checks.

Go Out in the Cold

Cold doors are a superior method of prospecting. That's right. Knock on 100 cold doors and you're bound to come up with at least one deal. How would you like to start out in the morning knowing that you'll have at least one deal that day? Everybody would. But everybody is not willing to work for it. The superstar is willing to knock on those doors. Why? Because superstars determine their own destiny. They, and nobody else, are going to decide how much money they're going to make.

Knocking on cold doors is not farming. Cold doors, to you, is a different area from your farm, if you have one. The cold door area is an area in which you're unknown. You may have driven through the area, but you never stopped.

"But Mike, I don't like people knocking on my door, so I'm not going to knock on doors." Okay, be poor. It's just that simple. Besides, how do you know whether or not people mind you knocking on their door until you actually do it? You don't know. You cannot impose your own view on prospects. That's one of the hardest things to learn. But learn it. Burn it into your brain. Do not assume how a prospect or client will respond. Chances are that you'll be wrong. The bottom line is this: How are you going to find people who want to list or buy property if you're not out there asking them?

You've knocked on the door. Someone has answered. You're a little scared. Nobody was supposed to be at home. Now what do you do? You look down into your quivering hand at your trigger card and read the first line. "Hi. I'm Bill Smith from Banana Realty. Do you mind if

I ask you a few questions?" Look up and smile now. Chances are that the prospect may take a little pity on you and smile back.

The prospect has only two answers available—yes or no. If the prospect says yes, your response is "Fine, thank you for your time," and move on to the next door. Remember, a deal is waiting for you out there; all you have to do is find it. You just found out that it wasn't at that house, that's all.

If the prospect says *no,* look down at your trigger card for the first question. "When do you plan on moving?"

Let's get to the heart of the matter, right? You want to list their house, so this piece of information is vital. You're discovering what their motivation for selling might be. If the prospect responds, "I have to move in four months," don't faint. You've got a live one. Their motivation to move is very high. Go for the listing presentation appointment.

On the other hand, if they respond, "I don't ever plan to move," their motivation is a lot lower. But don't despair. This person can still be a source—no, a veritable fountain—of information for you. Besides, *ever* has different meanings for different people. *Ever* for one person might mean six months; for another person, it might mean 20 years. You don't know what their meaning is, so go on.

Still smiling, look down at your trigger card for the second question. "How long have you lived here?" Pretty simple, right? Now listen to the answer. If it's a short time, they indeed might not want to move right away. If it's been more like 15 or 20 years, they might want to move. It all depends upon their motivation. There may be a second part to their answer, so make sure that you give them a chance to answer fully. You see, you don't know what they're going to say. Even if you think that you do, chances are you're wrong. So let them talk.

If they answer your second question with "None of your business," that's a pretty clear indication that they don't want to talk to you. What was the magic all-around word? "Fine." That's right. So you say, "Fine. Thank you for your time," and move on to the next house.

If everything has gone along pretty well with questions one and two, you move on to number three. "Where did you folks move from?" Are you making conversation? No. You are looking for leads.

What if they moved from 50 miles away, or even from out of state? Perhaps other members of their family want to move here as well. You may have just received a lead. You see, trigger cards free you to listen to what the prospect is saying so you can pick up as much information as possible. You don't have to worry about what to say next. Why? Because it's going to be one of two things. Either it's going to be the question written down on the trigger card, or it's going to be "Fine. . . ." Right?

The next question on the trigger card is: "How did you happen to pick this area?" What might you learn? You might hear a strong reason for someone to live in this area that hadn't occurred to you. You might even be able to use this same reason when trying to sell someone a house in the area! How did you get this reason? By listening and not worrying about what you would say next. Oh, the benefits of using trigger cards!

Question five: "If you were to move, where would you go next?" Listen carefully. What might you learn? No, you're not as interested in the location as you are in the motivation for moving. "Why would you be moving?" is really the question for which you're seeking an answer. But it's much less threatening to ask in this fashion.

Last question: "When would that be?" If they have to be gone in six months, you've got a real live prospect! If they're not leaving for a year, keep in contact with them on a regular basis, and make a tentative appointment for your listing presentation now. Why now? Because they should put their home on the market no later than six months before they have to move. Also, you're filling out your daily planner six months in advance, right?

These trigger card questions work. They have worked time and time again. What else do trigger cards accomplish? They help to establish your control of the situation and show that you are a professional.

Never tell prospects they have a beautiful house, dog or children. Your goal is to have them trust you enough as a professional to list their house, their biggest investment, with you to sell. They don't care what you think about their house, dog or children. They only care about how much money you can sell their house for, nothing else. You need to establish yourself as a real estate sales professional, not somebody from the neighborhood appreciation committee.

If you stand there at the door hemming and hawing and looking for something to say, they'll know—and you know—that you don't know what you're doing. You're wasting both your time and their time.

However, if you appear to be organized and efficient, then you're not wasting anybody's time and you'll get a listing.

Open Houses

One of my favorite topics is open houses. Holding an open house ranks right up there with having floor time; they're both generally a great waste of time. But since most sellers insist upon an open house, use it to your advantage.

First of all, chances are good that you won't sell that house. "But Mike, I held an open house and it sold." Miracles do happen. How many have you held where the house didn't sell? Most of the time.

So, what should you do during an open house? No, you shouldn't do a crossword puzzle, read a novel or watch a football game.

"But Mike, if I'm not doing those things, what will I *do?*" If you've been at the house for a couple of hours and nobody comes, you're going to close it up and leave. Of course, prior to arriving at the house you *have* put up eight or nine directional signs guiding people to the house, right? Don't keep an open house a secret if you want people to take a look. Announce it to the world!

There's a real estate company in the South that has about 900 signs up around town. That's right, 900. Guess what company you think of if you live in that town? Can you imagine 900 of your company's signs up around town? Guess how many listings this company has? No, it's not 900, not yet. It's 100. They have 100 listings and 900 signs up. Eight hundred of those signs direct people to the listings of the major streets. You must begin to think bigger if you're going to be earning that $100 per hour.

Now, back to the *real* reason why you hold an open house. You're looking for prospects. Prospects who will either list or sell property. "But Mike, I just want to sell that house." Remember, open houses generally don't sell the house. You have to think ahead for yourself and use the time to your advantage. Finding prospects is definitely to your advantage.

Who will come to an open house? The curious neighbor, someone who wants to buy a house and someone who is thinking about selling a house. All you have to do is find out which category people belong to and ask the right questions. I'm even going to give you the questions.

A word about how you should appear during an open house: You should be standing. Yes, standing at all times. Why? Because if you're seated in a comfortable chair, you'll begin to armchair-qualify buyers. This is a major mistake.

I have a friend who dresses very casually to go shopping. You know—jeans, shorts or maybe a very casual pair of pants. Salespeople usually don't even talk to him, because they prequalify him on the basis of how he is dressed. Mistake, mistake, mistake! He dresses that way to be comfortable. When he buys something, whether it's a pair of jeans, furniture or a car, he pays in cash. And he buys only better-quality merchandise. When was the last time you had a cash customer? Don't prequalify. Stand and greet people as they come through the door, okay?

Now to the questions. "May I show you through the home?", not "Take a look around." Why? Because you're going to be asking them questions as you go through the house with them. What else would you be doing? They all know what bedrooms, closets, kitchens and pools look like. You're gaining control.

"Do you currently live in the area?" will separate the curious from the buyers. But don't give up if they say that they live in the area. Maybe they want to sell. If you don't ask, you'll never know. Even if they don't want to sell, let them look through the house.

"Are you currently working with another broker?" This is a courtesy type of question. It shows that you're aware that they might be working with someone. Does it matter? No. Because if the agent were doing his or her job, they wouldn't be out going to open houses. They're fair game. They're prospects. They're why you're holding the open house.

"What would be the best time to show you property: weekends or weekdays?" Go for the appointment. Then make sure that you get their name, phone number, etc. How will you sell to them if you don't show them property? You won't. Get that appointment to show them what they're looking for and sell it to them.

Cold Calls

Cold calls on the telephone is not my favorite way to prospect; I prefer going to the door and being face-to-face. But if you're going to cold call on the telephone, realize that there is a higher incidence of rejection. It's easier for people to hang up the phone than to slam a door in your face. Use the same trigger card script that you would for cold doors, and realize that you'll have to talk to more than 100 people to get that deal. It's just that simple.

Sign Calls

Who is really on the other end of that sign call? Chances are that it's a curious neighbor. So, get them out in the open as soon as possible. How? Be direct. Try, "Which home in the area?" That ought to work.

If they don't own a home in the area, does that eliminate them? No, it doesn't. They may be thinking about selling. What could that mean to you? A listing.

"Mike, what happens if they don't live in the area?" Well, then, you just might have a real live prospect who wants to buy. It could be that house, or one of the houses you previewed that's in your inventory. That's why it's important to know what's on the market.

Walk-ins

Are you ready for walk-ins when they arrive? Take a look at your desk. Is it clean and organized? If not, clean and organize it.

Do you know what questions you're going to ask the walk-in? You have to find out what the prospects are looking for, their price range and what features they want. Then what are you going to do? You're going to take them out and sell them a house, because you'll show them what they want. Planning those questions makes it very easy.

I was in Hawaii awhile back and decided to buy a home there, because I was going there quite often for seminars. I walked into a real estate office, introduced myself and told them my price range and that I wanted a house on the ocean, or with an ocean view. I laid it all out for them. I told them that I would be back at three o'clock to look at three homes.

When I returned, this husband-and-wife team then took me out to look at three homes. Did any of the three have an ocean view? No. Were any of the three on the ocean? No. So, being my direct self, I said, "Do you have a problem? I told you what I wanted and none of these homes fulfills my requirements. Is it that difficult to find a home that has an ocean view or is on the ocean?"

I left them and went across the street to another real estate office, and I bought a home that afternoon. Don't make it hard on yourself; listen—and give prospects what they ask for.

Farming

What is farming? Farming is working a specific group of people or an area on a regular basis for the purpose of getting listings, sales or referrals. Key words here are "regular basis." That means you have contact with the people in the farm every 30 days. This does not mean leaving a card or flyer at the door. This means mailing a note, making a phone call, or a personal visit from you—not from some $3 per hour emissary.

Working a specific area is a waste of time unless you have a lock on it. "But Mike, I got two sales from my farm last year." Great. But how many total transactions were there within the farm? Twenty? Thirty? Two is not enough to justify the time necessary to work the area. In fact, if you aren't getting 20 to 25 percent of the business in that area, you're wasting your time. In terms of productivity, you'd be better off making cold calls. Do I have a solution? Of course.

Work a people farm. What is a people farm? It's any group or groups of people that you work on a regular basis. Who could constitute a people farm? Any group! FSBOs, the employees in a mall, a civic group, the people at your old job, the people at your spouse's job and so on.

How do you work this people farm? The same way that you would work an area farm—by note, call and personal visit. The great thing about a people farm is that they already know you—you don't have to go through the process of building their confidence. What an advantage!

How big should a people farm be? My goal was to have 1,000 people in my farm. The closest I ever got was 800; but compare that to the area farm of 225 homes and you can begin to see the advantages. By already knowing these people, you can more easily establish yourself as their real estate professional. More people means more opportunity to do business. More business means more dough. More dough means that you're becoming a superstar.

Did you know that 20 percent of all listings are tenant-occupied? That's a fact. What do you do when you come across tenants, just ignore them? No, not if you're a superstar—not if you're on your way to doing SIX.

These tenants are great prospects. Why? Because they're going to have to move; because they're used to living in a house; and because they're used to paying higher than normal rent. If you're previewing five homes a day, at least one will be tenant-occupied. It will pay you not to ignore them. Don't write them off just because they are renting. They may be unaware that they can buy a home with no money down if they're eligible for VA benefits. Work with them. How will you find out what they're going to do when the house sells? Ask them!

Try this: "When this home sells, are you planning to purchase a home or continue to rent?" That's simple and direct. If they say purchase, make an appointment to show them property. This is such a great business. There's only one thing you can do in this business, and that's make money.

Once you've sold a client a house, that's not the end of it. What more is there? What happens if they had to move and couldn't get the house they wanted? Well, six months to a year after the transaction closes, go back and see if you can't sell them the perfect house. Now you have the luxury of time to find the house they truly want.

"But Mike, the transaction got messed up and they were mad at me when it closed." They aren't going to be mad at you forever. Don't be afraid to go back to your past clients and see if they want to move, or if they know anybody who does. Start going back a week after it closes and ask, "Are you still mad at me?" If the answer is yes, tell them "Fine. I'll talk to you later." Just keep this up until they're no longer mad at you. Try going back every week or two to ask. You know, sooner or later they're going to begin to smile when they see you. Then is when you start working with them.

Better yet, you have a client who's happy with you and the home that he or she bought. Go back immediately, or even at the close, and ask if they know anybody who wants to sell a house. Be specific. "Do you know anybody at work who wants to sell a house, or who is looking for a house?" or, "Do you know anybody at your church . . .?" You get the idea. Help them jog their memory. The only thing it can do for you is make money. And that always sounds good to me.

You have just been presented with several ways to prospect—to look for those people who are either going to sell or buy property. If you were to do just a few of them on a regular basis, like once a week for a couple of hours, you couldn't help but be successful in real estate. It would be almost impossible for you not to be a superstar. So what are you waiting for? You know that you have the time, and now you know what to do with it! Get on to the SIX figures.

CHAPTER 4

Prospecting FSBOs and Expired Listings

Why do you recoil in fear at the thought of approaching a FSBO or an expired listing? That just doesn't make sense. These people are the only prospects in the world who tell you up front that they want to sell their property. You're now going to learn how to take advantage of this unique group of prospects.

This chapter covers the following topics:

- FSBO Fibs and More
- Why FSBOs Go FSBO
- The FSBO Lexicon
- Methods for Approaching the FSBO
- Why Do Listings Expire?
- Methods for Approaching the Expired Listing

FSBO FIBS AND MORE

It amazes me that more real estate agents don't stop at FSBOs. Why don't you stop? The list of reasons is almost endless:

"My brakes don't work."
"I don't have enough time."
"I'm not dressed correctly."
"Everybody has already stopped."
"I'm allergic to them."
"They probably aren't at home."
"It's Tuesday."

As the list goes on and on, the reasons get progressively funnier. What is the actual reason? You fear them. And you don't want the money. "But Mike, I want the money." Sure, you want the money, but you fear them more than you want the money. If that weren't the case, you would be the champion FSBO listener of all time.

So in order to earn all of that money, what do you have to do? Overcome your fear of these graduates of good ol' CU (You remember, Client University). I'm going to show you how to overcome that fear and list these people who want to sell their property. Listing people who want to sell their property . . . sounds difficult, doesn't it?

First of all, why do you fear the FSBO? Just like any other prospect, all the FSBO can ever really tell you is "no." Now that we have that established, why else do you fear the FSBO? Do any of these look familiar?

"We think they know what they're doing."

If they really knew what they were doing, they'd be selling real estate and making more money than you're making.

"If it's priced right, it will sell."

Sure. What are the chances that it's priced correctly? Maybe 10 percent. What does that mean? It means that even if it's priced right, you can do a better job of marketing than they ever thought of doing.

"I don't know what to say."

Well, we're getting closer to the truth. Just keep reading, and this reason will go straight to the trash can.

"They had a bad experience with a real estate person in the past."

Who cares? You're a real estate professional. If they didn't have that bad experience with you, it doesn't matter. You will have a plan of action to sell their house.

"They want to save money."

The complete statement is, "They want to save money and not pay a commission." But they will only save money if they sell their house. Let me tell you a little fact: according to the NATIONAL ASSOCIATION OF REALTORS®, 94 percent of all FSBOs list with a REALTOR®. Why do they list? Because they can't sell it themselves. You see, they can't do it without you.

"It's not a positive situation when we talk to them."

You know, if you were out there talking to them all the time, I could almost buy this reason. Nobody likes rejection or confrontation. However, in every group I've ever talked to, less than 5 percent talk to FSBOs on a regular basis. Another really interesting item is that that same 5 percent seems to be the ones who are becoming, or already are, superstars. They're the ones who are making $100 per hour.

Are FSBOs good prospects? You bet. Once again, they, and the expireds, are the only prospects in the world that you know for sure want to sell their property.

Another way to look at FSBOs is that they're part of the competition. You do preview property—other brokers' property, right? Well, FSBOs are just another broker's property. You need to add it to your inventory. So if you're out there looking at the FSBO property, what's to stop you from talking to him about listing it with you? Nothing.

WHY FSBOs GO FSBO

Has it ever occurred to you that FSBOs might be scared of you? That's right. All people have fears, and the FSBO may just be advertising his fear to you. Don't people sometimes get unnecessarily hostile in order to hide their fear?

What could a FSBO possibly be afraid of? Well, what happens if he or she lists with you and nobody shows up, neither you nor a prospective buyer? What happens if you sell it and the deal gets messed up while in process? What happens if you get an offer and it's lower than the FSBO thinks the house is worth? You see, the FSBO has a lot to be afraid of in his or her mind.

FSBOs might not really need to sell the property. They put a sign out, and if they get an offer that's $100,000 over market, they'll sell. Look, these people don't really want to sell, so you don't have to deal with them. However, you won't know this unless you're out there talking to them.

A FSBO may not want to pay any commission. That's fine, but remember that 94 percent of FSBOs eventually list with an agent to sell their property. What does that tell you? If the motivation is strong enough, they'll list. Ninety-four percent of them have strong enough motivation, according to NAR, so go out there and find them. Ninety-four out of 100 are going to list. Why not with you?

The FSBO is willing to pay a 3 percent commission. Wonderful. He or she wants to act as listing agent. Don't you have enough deals that get into trouble in escrow when you're working with licensed real estate agents? Why on earth would you want to risk even more problems? If you have a buyer for their property and they won't list it with you, forget them. Open the MLS book; there are other houses for sale by licensed brokers. Don't mess with the 3 percent FSBO. FSBOs who "just want to try it for a few days" are advertising for a real estate professional. When the right one comes along, they'll list. So get out there and find them.

What if the FSBO has had a bad experience in the past? Find out what happened and when it happened. Remember that you're a real estate professional, not some part-time dabbler. What if the problem occurred 20 or 30 years ago and the FSBO had to sell for less than the listed price? Could it possibly have been overpriced? Not a chance. We all know that when FSBOs list, their asking price is always the right price. Enough of that.

The FSBO's husband or wife is a great salesperson. But are they real estate sales agents? No? Then they do not know how to market a piece of property. When you talk to FSBOs and get beyond the reason they're going FSBO, the most important thing to find out is why they're selling their property. This "why" is their motivation. If they have to be out of town by sundown, they're motivated and are in sore need of your services. However, if they don't need to move at any specific time, they're not motivated. If they really don't know why they're selling their property, except that it seemed like the thing to do, they're not motivated. Unless you can motivate these people by getting them interested in another piece of property, don't mess with them. You will only be wasting your time.

THE FSBO LEXICON

Lexicon? What is a lexicon? A lexicon is "the special vocabulary of a field of study." Since we are studying FSBOs, words that are associated with them are especially important. You already know those words, but you may not think of them when you deal with or think of FSBOs.

The first word is *opportunity.* There's plenty of opportunity when you start prospecting FSBOs. Open the newspaper, especially the Saturday or Sunday newspaper. You'll find innumerable FSBOs, literally hundreds of them. What does this tell you? That you have a lot from which to work.

Competition is another word in the FSBO lexicon. You don't have any competition when prospecting FSBOs. Sure, you have those agents who talk to them once, briefly, and never go back. But are they really competition? No! Remember, less than 5 percent of all real estate sales agents prospect FSBOs on a regular basis. The field is wide open. Compared with other methods of prospecting, this sounds great to me.

Motivation: remember, motivation determines why they're selling the property and how fast it has to be sold. If their motivation is high and you can quickly determine what that motivation is, the better chance you have of listing the property. If they don't have any motivation, don't waste your time just for the sake of getting a listing. If you list a piece of property and the motivation of the seller is low, it probably won't sell. If it doesn't sell, you won't get a commission.

I knocked on the door of a FSBO in Huntington Beach. Just so you get the picture, the yard was a mess and the house was worse. It was filthy—one of the worst houses for sale I had ever seen. I asked the seller how much he wanted for the house. He said he wanted $98,000. I thanked him and left.

Driving up the street, I found another FSBO. Like any other real estate sales agent, I stopped. It had the same floor plan as the other house, except that this home was in immaculate, move-in condition. It had new landscaping and new paint inside and out. It was beautiful.

This seller was asking $94,000 for his home—$4,000 less than the dog up the street.

In talking with the seller, I asked him if he was aware that his neighbor wanted to sell, and if he knew the condition of the neighbor's house. He said that he was, and that he didn't understand it. I asked him if I could come back in about ten minutes and left to talk to the other FSBO.

I asked the first FSBO if he was aware of his neighbor's house, its condition and price. He said he was. So I asked him how he expected to get more for his house. He said it was very simple: His neighbor had to move and he didn't. Guess who I went back to see and list. Motivation is the key.

The fourth word of the FSBO lexicon is *fact-finding*. This process is nothing more than establishing yourself as the real estate professional. How do you do this? By asking questions. If you ask FSBOs questions to determine their motivation, then you can decide if you want to list their property.

Just a moment of digression. You are not under any kind of responsibility, either legal or moral, to list someone's property, even if they want you to. You list property to sell, not to feather your inventory. You choose the listings that you will take. Prospects really do not choose you; you choose them. This little fact is not mentioned in any of the courses at CU. In fact, you're rarely told this as a real estate agent. You're going to be the one who has to work with these people. If you don't think you can, walk away from the listing.

"But Mike . . . walk away from a listing?" Yes. If you cannot work with them, walk away. There are so many listings out there for the superstar that you can afford to walk away. "But what do I say?" Try, "I'm sorry, but I will not be able to take your listing." Then stand up and leave. This will blow all of their training at CU right out the door. This is especially important if the sellers are putting too many contingencies upon the sale of the property, or if you just don't like them. Just as prospects can say no to you, you can say no to them.

Persistence is the last word in the FSBO lexicon. What are the odds of getting the FSBO listing if you only go there once? None. If you're only going to stop at a FSBO once, don't stop at all. Don't waste your time.

To be successful with FSBO listings, you must stop every day. "Every day? But Mike, I was told to stop once a week." That's if you don't want the listing. If you do want it, you need to stop every day, or at least talk to them every day. "What do I say?" Does it really matter? No, just as long as you see or talk to them every day. If you don't, they will list with someone else.

"But Mike, what if they get mad?" Who cares? Are they your customers yet? No. So continue to go back until they're your customers. And believe me, FSBOs will figure out that your persistence will work for them when you list their house.

Another advantage to being persistent is that it will give you plenty of practice in talking with the dreaded FSBO. That practice will lead to confidence, which will make you a stronger FSBO listener. What will happen then? Your name will be mentioned in the courses at Client University. Now, that only happens to superstars.

METHODS FOR APPROACHING THE FSBO

You have made the decision to actively prospect the FSBOs. Congratulations. But you want to know how to approach them.

Let's start with the double-team approach. It's very basic and will build your confidence. Instead of going to the door by yourself, you take another agent with you. It's just that simple; remember, there's strength in numbers.

I went to Texas to lead a seminar. A real estate agent picked me up at the airport to take me to where the seminar was being held. Right across the street from the hotel was a FSBO! I said to the real estate agent, "This is great. Let's stop at that FSBO and get a listing appointment for you. We have some extra time." He declined and declined and declined. Get the picture?

The seminar started, and I began talking about FSBOs. I asked if any of the agents had been across the street to talk to the FSBO. Not a one! Nobody had ever stopped to talk to the seller. I had an idea.

I took the entire seminar on a field trip. Six hundred people walked through a large parking lot and across the street. They filled the driveway and the front yard, and spilled out into the street; it was great!

Well, I went up and knocked on the door. A lady answered, and I thought that she might have a heart attack when she saw those 600 people in her yard. I introduced myself and said, "These people are attending a real estate seminar. Would it be okay if they were to stop by and see you about listing your property?" She just kind of nodded, which I took for a yes, and I thanked her.

You know what? I was in Texas three months later, and that house was still FSBO. I wonder if any of those agents ever went back?

The office blitz is another approach you can utilize. What happens is this: One day the entire office devotes a day to FSBOs. This can be done on the company caravan or on an individual basis based upon a list that's drawn up at the office. Can you imagine a FSBO being approached by 27 agents, all from the same office?

You know what's going to happen. The FSBO will call the office complaining about this inundation of real estate agents. The "hero" will offer to come out and talk about it. Guess what happens when the "hero" arrives to talk? That's right, a listing presentation. Chances are that he will walk away from the FSBO with a listing. (Don't forget to rotate heroes.)

You can use the phone to approach FSBOs, but it's not as effective. I always preferred to talk face-to-face with FSBOs, because it would establish the relationship faster. However, I know you will probably use the phone, no matter what I say. Just realize that your chances of success greatly diminish if you're using the phone.

This is definitely a trigger card situation. First question: "Is this the party who's trying to sell his [her] home?" You must establish with whom you're talking. Wouldn't it be a waste of time if you went through the whole card and found out that you weren't talking to the right people, or that you were talking to tenants?

The next question should be: "Would you be offended if I took a look at your home today?" FSBOs want to say "No." This gives them a chance to do so, and it works in your favor. Try asking the question so the answer is a no. You see? You get to go over and look at their house. Simple!

My favorite way was to contact FSBOs at the front door, face-to-face. It works better. Anybody who has consistent success with FSBOs has it at the front door, not on the phone. "But Mike, what do I say?"

It's a trigger card! "Hello, my name is _____, with _____. We are doing a survey of all of the FSBOs in the area to determine the reasons they sell their homes themselves. Do you have a moment to answer a few questions?" If they say yes, go on to the survey.

FIGURE 4.1 FSBO Survey

Seller's Name _____

Address _____

FSBO Survey

1. Why are you selling?
2. Where are you moving to?
3. How soon do you have to be there?
4. How long have you owned this home?
5. How did you determine your sales price?
6. What methods are you using to market your property?
7. Are you prepared to adjust your price down when working with a buyer?
8. Why did you decide to sell yourself rather than list with a broker?
9. If you were to list, which firm would you list with?
10. How did you pick that particular firm?
11. If you were to list, what would you expect the firm to do to get your home sold?
12. Are you familiar with our company's 21-Point Plan of Action?
    (If they say, "No, What's that?")
    It's the 21 things we do to get a home sold. What would be the best time to show them to you?
    Would _____ or _____ be better?

If no, then say, "Fine. Would you be offended if I took a look at your home today?" If they refuse to let you in, go on to the next house.

The survey is shown in Figure 4.1.

If you listen to the answers to these questions, you will learn a lot. Questions 1, 2 and 3 all deal with the motivation of the seller. You may find that they really don't *have* any motivation for selling; if so, don't waste your time. You may find that they really don't want to move for a year, in which case you should stay in contact with them on a weekly basis.

The answer to question 5 will tell you if they're already working with a real estate agent. However, if the agent were that strong the house would be listed. It's just nice to have the information.

Question 7 really deals with whether or not they're willing to pay a commission, so pay attention.

The answer to question 11 should be included in your presentation of the 21-Point Plan of Action. Don't miss these items. They're literally telling you what to do if you expect to list the property. Don't mess up on this one!

FSBOs can be so simple, yet they're so neglected. Now you have some tools to go out there and work FSBOs. They're not to be dreaded; they're to be prospected!

WHY DO LISTINGS EXPIRE?

Expired listings are a special case. They have already been through one experience they perceive to be bad, so they might be a little hostile to any real estate agent. And the real kicker—they may perceive all real estate agents to be lazy.

The basic trouble with expired listings is that they probably haven't been taken by a superstar. That may sound a little harsh, but it's true. If a listing were going to be bad, a superstar would have walked away from it. Do you realize the strength your position would hold if you had refused to take a listing, they listed with someone else and it expired? You could literally walk back in and write your own ticket. Being a superstar is great!

A listing might expire because the property is in poor shape. Don't be afraid to tell the seller he needs to clean up his yard, or that a pool that has green water in it is not a strong selling point. If you don't, the listing might just expire, and who do you think the seller will blame? You. Just remember to use a little tact when talking to the seller about what he needs to do.

What happens if the price is too high on a piece of property? It isn't going to sell and the listing will expire. It's just that simple. So don't list it. Walk away. Once again, you can say no just as well as the client or prospect.

If the sellers don't know where they are going or when they have to be there, that indicates a general lack of motivation. Once again, if the motivation is low and you can't raise it by getting the sellers interested in another house, walk away.

Who decides if the location of a piece of property is bad? Generally, real estate agents do. Who should make that decision? The buyer. Let buyers decide for themselves; what you may perceive as a drawback may be a strength to the buyer. This is another reason listings expire.

If you only took good listings to begin with, there wouldn't be any expired listings. If you were only strong enough to walk away from sellers who either demanded too much from you or asked too much for their property, then expired listings would not exist. That sounds very simple, but it's the truth. Know when to say no to a listing. There are too many good ones to waste your time on bad ones.

METHODS FOR APPROACHING THE EXPIRED LISTING

Okay, so how do you approach these potentially hostile people? It's really pretty easy. You approach them as if they were FSBOs.

Start with the same introduction at the door as you did with the FSBO. "Hello, my name is _____ with _____ . We are doing a survey of all of the expired listings in the area to determine why they expired. Do you have a moment to answer a few questions?" Very simple. If the answer is yes, go on with the survey shown in Figure 4.2; if the answer is no, go on to the next house.

This survey will give you information on which to base your listing presentation, so you will need to listen to all of the answers carefully. Don't be afraid to write down what they're telling you. Whoever heard of a survey taker not writing the answers to the questions that were asked? It only makes sense.

FIGURE 4.2   Expired Listing Survey

Seller's Name _____

Address _____

Expired Listing Survey

 1. Is your home presently for sale?

 2. Would you be offended if I took a look at your home today?

 3. Why do you feel your home did not sell?

 4. How did you happen to choose the company you listed with?

 5. What did they do that you liked best?

 6. What do you feel they should have done?

 7. What do you expect from the next company you list with?

 8. Which company have you already selected?

 9. Did your previous company advertise on a regular basis?

10. Did they hold open house continuously?

11. Did they caravan the home regularly?

12. Did your company have a complete 21-Point Plan of Action for you?

13. When would be the best time to show you our company's Plan of Action? Would _____ or _____ be better?

The answers they give to questions 3, 5, 6 and 7 are very important. They will tell you what the other agent did not do and what the sellers will expect from anybody they list with in the future. Apply those answers to your listing presentation and Plan of Action.

Also, after looking at the answers to the survey, you may decide that you don't want to list their house. Once again, don't be afraid of not listing a house.

A word about using the telephone to prospect expired listings: Don't. You will be far more effective if you do the survey in person. They may be angry and hostile to all real estate agents, and it's much easier to hang up the phone than close a door in someone's face. The phone is impersonal, and what these people may need is a little personal care and advice. Can you see if their house is a wreck by using the phone? No. That may have been the reason their house did not sell. Get out there and see them in person.

Who are the only people in the world who tell you they want to sell their property before you ever talk to them? That's right, FSBOs and expired listings. And since less than 5 percent of you ever prospect them on a regular basis, they're an untapped source of commissions. The real question is, are you going out to prospect that gold? If you're working for that $100 per hour, you're working the FSBOs and expired listings.

CHAPTER 5

Qualifying for Faster Sales

When you're sick and go to see a doctor, what does the doctor do before he can determine how to help you? He asks a lot of questions. What does the attorney do before he decides whether or not accept your case? He asks a lot of questions. What does the real estate agent do when someone wants to buy a house? He immediately starts showing them property. What *should* the real estate agent do? ASK QUESTIONS!

This chapter covers the following topics:

- Qualifying Defined
- The Importance of Qualifying
- How To Qualify
- The Uncooperative Prospect

By reading and understanding this chapter, you will learn the questions to ask that will soon have you making SIX.

QUALIFYING DEFINED

Qualifying is nothing more than determining the motivation of a buyer and his or her ability to fulfill that motivation. How are you going to get that information? By asking questions.

When you go to see that doctor, what kind of questions is he going to ask you? Where does it hurt? How long has it hurt? What kind of pain is it? Those kind of questions sound familiar, right? What is the doctor striving to do? He is gathering information that will assist him in determining how to best help you. He is qualifying you.

When you go to see the attorney, what kind of questions would he ask? What happened? When did it happen? Who was involved? The answers to these and other questions will assist the attorney in determining if he can or wants to help you. What is the attorney doing? He is qualifying you.

THE IMPORTANCE OF QUALIFYING

Why do these other professionals spend so much time in the beginning qualifying their prospective clients? Because it will save them time later. If they find they cannot help you, they can tell you so, and perhaps recommend someone who can. Whatever they say, it will have one of two effects: Either they will endeavor to assist you, or they will get you out of their office. It's just that simple.

Why can't a real estate agent be the same way? The answer is that you can, but you have to learn what questions to ask to qualify your prospective clients. Spending a few minutes at the outset can save many hours of aggravation later.

What are you seeking to find out? You want to know if the person wants to buy today; not tomorrow, or next month, or in six months, but today. That's called MOTIVATION.

Motivated buyers will want to buy as soon as you have found the right property for them. If your buyer is not motivated, he or she will always have an excuse for not buying, no matter what you do.

In addition to motivation, you want to know if the buyer has the ability to buy. That means, does the buyer have the money to make the purchase? The money can be in the form of cash, or down payment plus the ability to make monthly mortgage payments. How are you going to find this out? By asking.

You see, once you get the answers to a few simple questions, you know whether or not you can help a client. "But Mike, I just don't feel comfortable asking a lot of questions." Are you comfortable being poor? Probably not, so follow my advice and ask questions. If you don't ask questions, you're going to waste a great deal of time and have nothing to show for it in return.

Why does the doctor ask questions? Why does the attorney ask questions? To assure themselves that what they're doing is going to be profitable to them. If you're on your way to making $100 per hour, your time is at least as valuable as a doctor's and more valuable than most attorneys'. So don't be afraid to ask a lot of questions.

In addition to discovering buyers' motivation and ability, you can ascertain their needs, wants and desires by asking the right questions. This will separate the wishers from the buyers. Some people wish that $75,000 could buy a beachfront home in Southern California, but it can't. That's not even a down payment! It would, however, make a nice down payment on a condominium 40 miles inland.

A buyer may desire to live at the beach. He or she may want a four-bedroom, two-bath house with a pool, and may actually need a three-bedroom condominium. You must be able to separate their needs, wants and desires so you won't waste time. How are you going to do this? That's right, by asking questions.

What else will you accomplish by qualifying your buyers? You will establish yourself as a professional. By asking questions, you will not be talking to them about pie-in-the-sky houses but about what they can afford to buy today. If you're dealing with serious buyers, they will appreciate this. They will respect you because you're not wasting their time or yours, and losing money.

What do you do if you find that you're not dealing with a serious buyer? Say goodbye. Your time is too valuable to waste. Don't be afraid to tell them to come back when they're serious about purchasing real estate. Remember, if you're out there prospecting every day, you're going to come across more buyers than you could ever handle. What kind of power will that give you? The power to say goodbye! When you have the power to say goodbye, you will establish yourself as a professional. So if you don't have that backlog of buyers, start prospecting so you get one.

By qualifying buyers before showing them property, you're going to gain their respect. And if they respect you, you will have control. Sound too good to be true? It isn't. Most buyers think that buying a house is just a matter of looking at houses until they find one they like. If you're able to demonstrate to them that there's more to it than that, you will gain their respect as a professional. You will gain the same kind of control that a doctor or attorney exerts over clients. Doesn't that sound good to you?

HOW TO QUALIFY

Now that you understand some of the reasons you must qualify your buyers, it's time that you knew the important questions to ask.

Remember, there are only two kinds of buyers: those who know what they want and those who haven't the foggiest notion. Both of these buyers can be serious buyers; they're just approaching the problem from different perspectives. Part of your qualifying will be finding out what the buyer wants or assisting him or her in making a decision.

The first thing you will need to do is to introduce yourself. I know this sounds obvious, but you would not believe how many real estate agents do not introduce themselves to prospective clients. "But Mike, my name is on my name tag." Great! So how many people read name tags, and just how professionally are you acting if you don't tell them your name?

Because you introduce yourself, your prospective clients will introduce themselves to you. It's almost a reflex action in most people. "Hi. I'm Bill Smith. How may I help you?" If you stand, smile and extend your hand, what do you think prospective clients will do? They will smile, extend their hand and say, "Hi. I'm John Buyer and this is my wife, Mary. We want to buy a house." I know this is pretty tricky, but it works 99 percent of the time.

Once you have found out what they want, what do you do then? Do you figure out how you're going to spend your commission check? No. You ask those wonderful qualifying questions. It doesn't matter how they came to be in your office, whether by sign call, ad call or walk-in. You must qualify all buyers before showing them a single piece of property.

What are you going to say? Try, "John and Mary, there are a few questions I need to have answered before I can show you property. By answering these questions, I'll know what kind of property to show you." Most prospective clients will respond positively to this approach. You're communicating to them that your time is valuable; that you're a professional; and that you're interested in meeting their needs as quickly as possible. You're also beginning to establish control.

Here's a convenient tip. Type questions out on company letterhead and get them copied. Then whenever you need to use one, you'll have it at hand. You can either ask the questions yourself and write down the answers, or you can hand the sheet to the prospective buyers to fill out in the office. Now, on to the qualifying survey.

Is this your first visit to our city? You need to know this. If it's their first visit, give them a tour of the city. Why? Because you will eliminate the objection that they're not familiar enough with the city in the event that you find a house for them that day.

Where are you from? Use some common sense with this question, okay? If the answer to the first question was that they have lived in the city for 17 years, don't ask this question; just skip it.

How long have you folks been looking for a house? You're beginning to look for their motivation—their reason for buying. What if they answer, "This is our first day. We were just transferred to the area." Would you call that high motivation? I would. They need a home!

However, if they answer, "Oh, about six months," you'll want to find out why they haven't found a home yet. The best way to do this is by just asking, "Why haven't you folks found a home yet?" They come back with, "Well, nobody has asked us to buy." Ask them to buy when you get them to a house. In fact, as a general rule of thumb, always ask the buyer to buy. Every house you show them should be accompanied by a request to buy. It's not going to hurt you, and you may even get an unexpected sale. You can be lighthearted or sickeningly serious every time you ask, but ASK.

How many children do you have, and what are their ages? The answer to this question will begin to give you some idea of their needs. Mr. and Mrs. Buyer have come into the office because of an ad for a three-bedroom condo, but they have five children at home. Will a three-bedroom condo meet their needs? No, so you know you're going to have to look in a different direction for them. They will be needing four, five or even six bedrooms.

Where do you live now? You want their exact address. Why? So you can send them a follow-up note thanking them for coming in.

How long have you lived there? This is the perfect follow-up question! What do you think you're beginning to find out about now? That's right, equity. Let's say they answer "Twenty-five years." You're thinking, "Lots of equity." Cautionary word here: *Maybe* they have lots of equity. Wait until you have the answer to the next question.

Do you own or rent? Now, if they say "Rent," and they have lived at the same address for 25 years, have they built any equity? No. But if they have owned the house for 25 years, chances are they do have "lots of equity."

How is the resale market in your area? If they tell you it takes at least six months to sell a house, you need to find out if their house is for sale now. They may not be in a position to buy from you today, because they may need to sell their home first.

Why do you think it's important for you to know if they're in a position to buy from you today? Because you can make money faster by selling houses than by listing them, generally. If they can't buy from you until they have sold their house, you may not want to spend very much time with them today. However, if your company has a referral system, perhaps you can refer them to a person in their area and collect that referral fee. This way you will be able to stay in closer contact with them, and you're building the relationship.

What if they say, "You put a sign up in the front yard and it's gone the same day"? Ask them if they have a sign up in their yard. If not, go after the referral. Now you're beginning to get the idea.

Where are you employed? I know it sounds stupid, but you're just seeing if they have a job. Occasionally, a person will come along who doesn't have a job and wants to buy a house. It sounds ridiculous, but it happens. Save yourself a little aggravation and ask.

How long have you been employed there? You're beginning to think about the lender with this question. What if the answers to the last two questions tell you that he has worked at a fast-food place cooking hamburgers for two weeks. Do you think he might have a tough time getting a loan? If he doesn't have the ability to pay for a house, he can't buy a house, no matter how motivated he might be to do so. You've got to be able to tell him that, in a fashion that won't create ill will.

What if the last two answers indicate that the buyer has been employed by the same company for the last 20 years and that he is a vice-president? It ought to be pretty easy for this buyer to get a loan.

What is your position with the company? You're trying to get an idea of how much money they make. If you get an answer such as, "I'm the president of a large multinational corporation," chances are you don't have a no-money-down buyer on your hands.

Can you begin to see the great tool this survey is for qualifying buyers? If you use this kind of survey, you will be showing fewer homes to more buyers and making more sales. "Wait a second, Mike—more buyers? Where did they come from?" That's the beauty of a qualifying survey. You will be working more efficiently; you will have more time to work with buyers because you will only be working with motivated people who have the ability to buy. More time. More buyers. More money!

Have you seen any homes that you like? You know what happens here? You compare this answer with the answer to the third question. This is a little double-check on the information they're giving you.

You see, if they told you in response to that question that they just started looking for a house, and here they tell you they have seen a lot of houses they like, you could suspect that they were not being totally honest. What do you think your response should be in this situation? No response. Just keep it in mind that you will have to establish firm control to work with these people. You will have to become their expert.

How soon will you be able to move if we find the right home? There's a tendency not to ask this question, but you *need* to ask it. Why? Because its answer clearly establishes buyer motivation. That motivation will be out on the table for the whole world to see when the buyer answers this question.

"We couldn't possibly move until school is out in June, which is six months from now." No motivation. There's nothing more for me to say about these people, except that I would not spend a lot of time with them today.

"We have to move immediately. The sale of our house closes in 30 days. We need to buy today and close in 30 days." That's great motivation. It's okay to begin to visualize the commission check, just don't go out and spend it.

Oh, by the way, are you working with any other brokers in the area? Don't be afraid to ask this question. You know they probably are working with other agents and brokers, so let's just get it out in the open. Why? You do want to sell them a house, don't you? Of course. By asking this question, you will be moving toward a position of control and exclusivity. The buyer will think you're really a strong agent if you're willing to bring it up. This is not a technique they teach at good old CU.

If you're comfortable doing this, ask for a commitment from the buyer to work with you exclusively. Why not? You do want to make money, don't you? You do want to be in control of the situation, don't you? So ask. What have you got to lose? Chances are you will be the only agent to bring up the topic of other brokers and the request for exclusivity. It will just strengthen your position.

Here's how you can ask for their allegiance.

"I preview homes every day. Every day I'll be out there looking for a home for you. If I'm going to take this time to work for you, will you make a commitment to buy your home from me? This means that if you're driving down the street and you see another broker's sign on a house that you're interested in, you'll call me and I'll get the information for you. If you go into an open house and like it, you'll call me to present the offer or find out more about the house. If I commit to you, then you commit to me."

That's easy to say and it's nonthreatening. You're asking to become their expert in real estate for that area. You're pledging to work on their behalf to find them a house. You're going save them countless hours of frustration working with various real estate agents. You're going to be their hero. The only catch is that you'd better come through and remain in constant and daily contact with them. That sounds easy enough.

How much time do you have to look at property today? Once again, you're recognizing that they may be working with other agents. If they say they have another appointment in a couple of hours, chances are the appointment is with another agent. So what do you do?

Offer to call the other agent and tell them that Mr. and Mrs. Buyer might be a little late. This is not a tough thing to do and will increase your standing in the buyers' eyes. You'll gain more control.

How long have you seriously been looking for a home? If they have been looking for a year with other agents, get rid of them. Of course, if you like frustration and the opportunity to get an ulcer, try to work with them. My advice is to find some new buyers.

If for some reason you want to work with them, get a commitment from them that they will buy a house if you can show them the kind of house they're looking for and if they can afford it. If you cannot get a commitment, throw away the lead card. They lack motivation.

Also lacking motivation is the buyer who is looking for the perfect house. As you can see, you may need to spend more time prospecting for buyers. If you have more buyers than you can handle, it becomes very easy to say goodbye to the nonmotivated buyer. Believe me, if you're following my instructions, you're going to have more buyers than you can handle. You're going to be achieving a SIX-figure income.

How many bedrooms will you need? Now you're getting down to what they need. Another of Mike's little hints—ask the wife. She will be the one making the decision on the needs. When the wife decides that it's time to buy a house, a house will be bought. She will also decide what house the couple will buy.

A couple was recently looking at a house that the husband wanted to buy because it was a "good buy." The wife looked around the house and then looked at him. "You say 'good buy' now, but every morning you'll say goodbye to me, and I'll be stuck in this house. No way!" They did not buy the house. Talk to the wife!

If they own a home: *How much will you realize from the sale of your home?* Listen to this answer. As you do, think about the market. Are sellers getting their asking price, or less? Depending upon market factors, it might be wise to discount what the buyers tell you by 10 to 15 percent.

Will it be necessary to sell your home to buy the next one? If it has to be sold and you find them their dream house, you may have to assist them in arranging a swing loan or some kind of creative financing. If they do not have some other strong motivating factor, you may want to say "see you later" without creating ill will.

If we find the perfect home today, are you in a position to buy it? If the answer is no, then move on to the next buyer. These people lack motivation. You do want to get paid for the work you do, right? If you work to find them the perfect home and they can't buy it, you will just be wasting your time. You might as well go to the beach or golf course.

How much of your savings will you be able to invest in your new home? You're talking about the down payment with this question. Of course, if they're going to be using the proceeds from the sale of their existing home, you will need to add the amount from savings to calculate the total down payment. This is the first of several financial qualifying questions.

What price range have you been considering? The buyers may not have a clue as to what prices really are, or what they can afford. You may need to help them. Don't be afraid to do this and to be honest about what they can afford. It will ultimately put you in a stronger position.

What is the most you can afford to pay monthly? By looking at their down payment and figuring in their monthly payments, you will be able to determine if they have a realistic price range, or what their price range should be.

What do you like about your current home? Listen carefully and write it all down. They will be looking for a lot of these items in their new home. Use this as a shopping guide when previewing homes.

Describe your perfect home. Again, write these items down. The above list is a shopping guide; this is a wish list. Your goal here is to cross off as many things as possible. What? Yes, cross them off.

Let's say Mr. and Mrs. Buyer's dream home would be a two-story, four-bedroom, two-and-a-half-bath colonial style with a pool and rose garden in the back yard. Oh, yes, it must have a circular driveway. Now start asking them questions. "If the home we found had everything else but was only one story, would that be okay? You only have one child; if we found a three-bedroom, two-bath house you really liked, would that be okay? What would happen if the location was perfect, but it was a ranch style? Would it be okay if there was no pool, but there was room for one?" You get the idea.

So what does this do for you? The buyers have already handled their own objections. Say that Mr. and Mrs. Buyer are in a home they both really like. All of the buying signals are there. Suddenly Mr. Buyer says, "Honey, this house has only three bedrooms." You can take out your list and say, "Mr. Buyer, you told me that three bedrooms was okay. You see, it's crossed off the list." Objection handled. It's just about time to write up that offer!

Are you working with one mortgage banker or lender exclusively yet? No? Well, get one. This person can save you a lot of time and aggravation. What can he do to help you qualify buyers? He can prequalify them financially. It's great, because then you will know exactly what the buyer can afford.

"But Mike, will lenders do this?" Yes, and they love to do it. Why? Because it will give them the inside track when you sell the buyers a home and they need a loan.

Here's what you need to do: Talk with the lender and explain that you will have all of your buyers contact him or her for a financial prequalification before you show them houses. Then have the lender call you with price range information. You will know exactly what the buyer can afford.

You know what else this will do for you? It will further establish you in the minds of the buyers as a professional and will ultimately lead to more control. And if the lender tells you the buyers cannot qualify for a loan for a home, you won't waste your time even going through the qualifying questions.

Where should you qualify buyers? You can do it in your office or their home. You can attempt to do it over the phone, but it's not as effective as doing it in person. *Never* try to qualify a prospective buyer in the car. It just doesn't work. You will give up any position of strength or control, because your attention is divided.

THE UNCOOPERATIVE PROSPECT

Some buyers will refuse to answer any qualifying questions or talk to a lender prior to coming in to your office. What do you do?

Mike Ferry's policy on qualifying: If a prospect refuses to answer any of the qualifying questions, DON'T SHOW HIM OR HER PROPERTY. It's that simple.

If you're prospecting correctly, you're going to have more buyers than you can handle. If you don't have a backlog of buyers, spend more time prospecting until you get one. By qualifying your buyers, you will be selling more homes faster. More homes means more money. More money means that you're getting closer to $100 per hour, and isn't that your goal?

So if a prospect will not answer the qualifying questions, refer him or her to another agent—to one of the $10 per hour people who like to waste time.

Remember, you're a real estate professional—every bit as professional as the doctor or attorney. You're a specialist when it comes to the sale of homes; nobody does it better. Being a professional, you want to utilize your time in the most efficient manner possible, because for you, time is really money.

Like the attorney and doctor, you must ask a series of questions before you can determine whether or not you should assist a person in buying a house. You qualify your prospects so that you will not waste any time—and by qualifying them, you're selling faster. You're getting closer and closer to $100 per hour—closer to that SIX-figure income.

CHAPTER 6

Superstar Showing Techniques

Now that you've got a certified and qualified buyer that you obtained by prospecting, what do you do? You show the buyer property!

This chapter covers the following topics:

- Secrets to Showing Property
- Making It Easy for the Client To Buy
- The Importance of Questions

Now that you have done the work and found the buyer, learn what to do with him or her to earn a commission check.

SECRETS TO SHOWING PROPERTY

These methods *must* be secrets, or else everybody would be using them and earning more money, right? Learning these points will put you that much closer to earning SIX.

Here is an easy tip to follow: Always show your personal listings first. If the buyers want a colonial and you have a ranch-style home in your inventory that meets the basic requirements for size and price, SHOW IT! Who knows? They might just buy it, and you make more money.

Do you know what else is nice about selling your own listings? It becomes unbelievably easy to work with the other agent, because the other agent is you. Those are big advantages to showing your own listings first.

Don't take anything with you except the contract when you show property. Why should you take the contract? So you can write the offer on the spot. What do you need for a buyer to buy a house—the MLS book? Office stationery? Listing presentation trigger cards? NO. Just the contract.

I once showed property to a couple all day. Finally, at about 5 P.M., we were in a house that I asked them to buy, and they said yes. I had a sale, but I didn't have a contract, so we went back to the office to fill it out. But when we got back to the office, the buyers began to have some doubts. They wanted to go back out to the house. No problem, I wanted them to be happy.

We went back to the house and the buyers doubts were satisfied. Did I bring the contract with me? No. So we went back to the office, and once again the buyers had questions about the house that necessitated a return trip.

As a matter of fact, we went back to that house four times. The last trip was made at 9 P.M. The buyers had wanted to buy at five o'clock, yet four hours later I still didn't have a signed contract. Why? Because I didn't take it with me in the first place. You can bet that by the time we made the last trip I had the contract with me ready for their signatures.

The contract is the item that's most important to you getting the sale and that commission check.

Another one of those "secrets" is that you must work hard to sell the sellers. This means that you have to remind them that you need their assistance to sell their house. Ask them to open the drapes or to make sure the house is clean. Remember, a clean pool makes for an easier sell than a green one. If necessary, remind them that you want to sell their house as much as they want it sold.

Here is a tough one: Learn to give buyers what they want. If they insist upon having a swimming pool, make sure that every house you show them has a swimming pool. This is obvious, but we don't always remember it.

Many industries in America would profit if they just paid attention to what the customer wanted, instead of dictating what the customer will get. Perhaps that's why America, as an industrial nation, has fought an uphill battle in recent years to regain preeminence. Learn from other people's mistakes: Give customers what they want. It will make your job so much easier.

The last of the secrets is: Make it easy for the customer to buy from you. Earl Nightingale said that salespeople should look at all customers and see "MMFI" stamped on their foreheads. MMFI stands for Make Me Feel Important. Isn't that what we all want—to be made to feel important? This is one way you can make it easy for customers to buy: Make them feel important.

The customer—the buyer—really is important if you're expecting to get a commission check, right? So make them feel important by listening to what they want and giving it to them.

Another way to make buyers feel important is to let them decide if they want to buy or not. That sounds ridiculously simple; but how many of you prejudge your buyers as to whether or not they can afford to buy a particular house—or even if they should buy a house at all? Let buyers decide for themselves.

MAKING IT EASY FOR THE CLIENT TO BUY

What does "Making It Easy for the Client To Buy" mean? It means making it easier for the customer to say yes. Everything in this list of things to do has one thing in common: to assist you in selling a house and getting to those magic SIX figures. This section could be retitled "Making It Easy To Sell a House."

Call first before showing property. Don't just show up on the sellers' doorstep; use some common courtesy and call them first to make an appointment to show their house. Wouldn't it be embarrassing if a party was going on when you arrived at the house with your buyers? Don't think it doesn't happen, because it does.

"But Mike, what if I'm driving down the street and the buyers see a sign on a house that they want to inspect?" You stop the car, go up to the door, introduce yourself to the owners and tell them that you have buyers in the car who would like to look at their house. Ask them if now would be okay, or if it would be better for you to come back later, and name a time. That will probably get you and your buyers in to see the house.

I know this situation is unavoidable at times, but don't make a habit out of it. You should know what your buyers want through your prequalifying questions, and you should arrange to show them houses that best meet their needs. Keep impromptu showings to a minimum. Also, it's a good idea to call the selling broker from your car phone, if you have one. Selling agents may not appreciate your going directly to the seller.

Always call and explain why you didn't show property when you had arranged to do so.   You're making arrangements ahead of time with the sellers, right? Your buyers decide to buy the first house that you show them (don't laugh, it happens), so you don't show them any other houses. Get back to the other sellers and tell them what happened. It's just common courtesy.

You need to have the sellers' cooperation if you're going to sell their houses. It's just as important to have communication with them as with your own clients. What happens if you make arrangements with them to show their house and you do a "no-show"? Do you think they will be as cooperative the next time you call? Maybe not. Learn to communicate with the sellers. Remember, you're indirectly working for every seller, even those who are not direct clients. Each seller is a potential commission check.

Ask questions in the car while showing property.   These questions are not about their last vacations, or how they're doing in the stock market. Who do you have in the car with you? Buyers. So what do you think the general topic of the questions should be? That's right, buying real estate. You want to keep them thinking about buying. This is just another method of exerting control.

Try a question like this: "If we found a house today and you fell in love with it, but it required an additional $5,000 in down payment than you were prepared to pay, would you even consider it?" This gets them thinking and talking. And when buyers talk, you learn—that is, if you're listening. Do you begin to understand why listening is so important?

If buyers are motivated to buy, keep showing them property until they do.   Don't show them three houses and then stop. If buyers want to buy, they will buy from somebody. Why not you? They'll buy from you if you continue to show them property.

Show buyers houses in groups of three.   Why? Because buyers will become confused if you show them more than three at a time. Show three and try to close on one. If they don't want to buy any home you've shown them, show them three more and try to close. If they are motivated to buy, keep going until you sell them.

A few years ago I was showing houses to a couple who had been transferred to Southern California from Florida. They wanted to buy and move into a home in seven days. Were they motivated? Yes. I showed them property from 9 A.M. to 9 P.M.

I showed them a total of 27 homes. Note that 27 is a multiple of three: they saw nine groups of three homes each. I showed them three homes and tried to close; then I showed them three more homes. What did I get for my effort? A commission check.

Select the scenic route to the home.   If you're showing someone a $250,000 house, don't go through a neighborhood of $90,000 homes. And the reverse is true as well: Don't go through a neighborhood of $250,000 homes with a VA or FHA buyer; it will only serve to discourage him or her.

What should they see on this route? The amenities. Show them schools, churches, shopping centers, etc. Buyers today are as interested in the amenities as they are in the home itself; sometimes these amenities are even more important than the house.

Don't oversell the house before showing it to the buyer.   Do you know why this happens? Because we force our expectations and point of view on the buyers. Don't do that! It doesn't matter what you think about a piece of property. Your opinion should never enter into the conversation with the buyer.

What happens if you describe a house as the most beautiful that you have ever seen, and the buyer doesn't think so when you get there? The buyer is let down. Even if the house really does meet all of the buyer's requirements, he or she will be disappointed, and you won't get a commission check.

What's the rule? Don't oversell the house before the buyer sees it. This means that you must stay away from comments such as, "This is the most beautiful house I've ever seen," or "You'll love the view from the family room." Let the buyer make these discoveries. I'll tell you how to help buyers see these things for themselves later.

As quickly as possible, separate the lookers from the buyers. What are you really looking for? You're looking for the buyers. "But Mike, how do I look for buyers? I've already asked them all of the qualifying questions. What more can I do?"

Watch your clients very carefully. What will you see? You'll see their reactions to the houses you show them and you'll hear their comments. If they keep walking around the kitchen marveling at everything they see and are making those positive cooing sounds, chances are you have buyers on your hands. If you hear a comment like "We love the neighborhood," you're talking to buyers.

If you see a customer measuring the living room or the bedroom, you're watching a buyer in action. What do you do? You ask for the sale. How simple.

> "Will this living room accommodate your furniture?"
> "Yes."
> "I guess we better write up an offer."

This isn't too tricky, is it? Be direct. Remember that you only get paid when a house sells, not for showing a house—so sell houses. Every house that you show should be accompanied by the question, "Do you want to buy this house?"

"But Mike, if they don't want to buy the house, they might get upset when I ask them." So? You're not always going to see those buying signals and hear those cooing sounds. Some buyers are just unemotional. They may want to buy but are just waiting to be asked. You'll never know for sure unless you ask them, and who knows? You might just sell a house with a lot less effort than you expected.

What happens if they refuse to buy every home you show them? Assuming that you're meeting all of their requirements, you may be dealing with lookers. Don't waste time with these people; be up front with them. "Mr. and Mrs. Buyer, if we find the perfect home today, will you buy it?" Be direct and to the point.

If they're always finding an excuse not to buy, refer them to another agent and get the referral fee. You may not have been able to gain their confidence; perhaps somebody else can.

If you feel as though they will never buy, do yourself and your associates a favor and send them on their way. Sure, it takes guts, but all you're doing is losing money by continuing to deal with them. You're on your way to SIX; you don't have time to deal with lookers. "Mr. and Mrs. Buyer, I don't think that I'm going to be able to sell you a house right now. When you're ready to purchase a home, please come back and I'll be happy to work with you." It's plain, simple and to the point.

Always park across the street from the house.   Don't park in the driveway so the buyers won't see the run-down house next door. They will see it sooner or later. Better that they see it with you rather than have a deal fall apart later.

Why do you park across the street? So the buyer will see the neighborhood and the entire house. Use some common sense, though; if the house is set back a quarter of a mile from the street, go ahead and pull in the driveway. When in doubt, common sense should prevail.

As you approach the front door, say to the buyers, "Let's look at this home as if it were vacant."   This is a great idea, and I have to admit that I got it after doing some research. Generally, most homes are nicely decorated. Where do those furnishings go when the house is sold? That's right—with the seller, in most cases. So the house the buyers are seeing is not the one that they will be buying. This will assist the buyer in making a decision.

This same technique will work very well for homes that are hideously decorated. You know the kind I'm talking about—homes in which the colors don't match or complement each other. The kindest thing you can say about them is that they're decorated in an eclectic fashion. It's just as important that buyers look at these homes as if they were vacant so they get a true view of the house.

Once inside the front door, tell the buyers, "Let's make ourselves at home. I'm here just to answer questions."   This will help prevent buyers from becoming too emotional at the beginning. If buyers start out too excited, they will peak too soon, and by the time they have seen the entire house they will be flat. You've got to help pace the buyers' response if you want them to buy.

Keep the buyers together inside the house.   This may sometimes be a little difficult. Why do you think this is important? You really don't think they're going to run off with the silver. It's important because it's a way for you to maintain control. You want to show them the house.

What will happen while you're showing them the house? You will probably hear comments and see gestures that will tell you whether or not they like it. Also, you'll have the opportunity to turn what they might perceive as negatives into positive attributes of the house.

What would you say if the house backed up to a very busy street? Tell them that a busy street is safer and more secure than a secluded residential street. That's true. What happens if the house has a messy, unkempt back yard? Ask the buyers to use their imagination to create any kind of yard they want. If you don't say these kinds of things, buyers will see only what is there. And if they aren't with you, how are you going to hear their comments or see their expressions?

Try to save something good for last, but show it to them first.   I know this sounds confusing, but it's simple. If the buyers want a pool, take them through the house and show them the pool first. Let them make some cooing sounds, and then show them the rest of the house. Make sure that the last thing that you show them is, once again, the pool, and let them make some more cooing sounds.

What will this do? This will reinforce the positive points of the house. The first and last things they see are positive: They want a pool and you're showing them a pool. Remember one of the hints? Get the seller to help you sell the house. A clean pool will sell better than one that's green.

Get the customer emotionally involved with the house.   Nobody, but nobody, buys a house on logic. "But Mike, what about the person who buys because it's a good buy?" That's greed, not cold logic. Your job is to get buyers excited about the house.

Buyers might buy because the house has a nice kitchen or shop area. That's emotion. It's the warmth of the kitchen and visions of family unity that might be selling the house. Or it may be because they have always wanted a workshop area to build furniture or invent a better mousetrap. You see, you're selling dreams and emotions, so the important thing to do is find out which dreams and emotions are important to the buyer and key in on those.

Be enthusiastic.   Note that I didn't say "Try to be enthusiastic." Enthusiasm is a must, because you will communicate it to the buyer. If you aren't excited about houses and selling them, how can you expect the buyer to be enthusiastic? You can't! So don't be afraid to smile or to show that you like what you're doing.

It's so much easier to sell houses with a smile and a little enthusiasm than it is with a frown. Who wants to make a momentous purchase from someone who is grumpy? Nobody does. So smile and be confident.

The better you know the product and the more you know how to sell, the easier it is to be enthusiastic. Enthusiasm is nothing more than having product information, being able to communicate that information and being excited about it. Don't be afraid to like what you're doing and to let it show.

Let buyers take notes while you're showing them property. Give the buyers a pad of paper and a pen and ask them to write down everything they do not like about the house. The beauty of this idea is that they're writing down their objections. If you handle the objections, you've got a sale!

"But Mike, what happens if they don't write anything down?" That's even better, because that means they love the house—there isn't anything they don't like about it. What do you do then? You write up the contract and get a commission check.

Always take one car, even if it's theirs. How are you going to talk with them, win their confidence and keep them thinking about buying if you're not in the same car? You're not. So take one car and maintain control.

Never make a statement, only ask questions when showing property. This goes right back to not forcing your point of view on the buyer. I cannot overstate the importance of this. Keep your views to yourself!

How do you do this? Instead of saying, "What a beautiful living room," ask, "Do you like the living room?" Get the buyers involved. If you simply make a statement, then the buyers don't need to respond; they can just kind of grunt. Is that what you want? No, you want buyers to respond and get emotionally involved with the house. The buyer could even say, "This is the ugliest living room I've ever seen." That's great! At least you know what the buyer is thinking.

If you know what the buyer is thinking, then you can maintain control. How else are you going to know what is on the buyer's mind if you don't ask? Ask questions; don't make declarations. Just use simple questions and you will maintain control.

THE IMPORTANCE OF QUESTIONS

Selling is nothing more than asking questions. You see, once you answer buyers' questions, they should be ready to buy.

What are you going to learn from the answers to your questions? You will learn their needs and desires. You will find out if they like what you're showing them—and if they don't, why. And most important, if you ask, you will find out if they will buy.

Remember that an answer to a question, even if it's negative, will help you, because you'll learn something from the buyer. You may hear, "No, I don't like it." That's okay; now you know what the buyers don't like. You will also learn what they like, so you'll either be able to sell them that house or you'll know better what to show them.

What's happened? You've gotten the buyers involved emotionally with the house. When buyers are involved emotionally, you have more control.

When you ask questions, you keep yourself and the buyers on track. What track should you be on? You're on a sales track, and don't get off until you have the house sold or you move on to a different house.

Again, the more you ask questions, the more you know what buyers are thinking. If you know what buyers are thinking, you will have more control. Knowledge is control. These aren't pushy or hard questions; you're going to learn more from simple questions that require an answer. Will their furniture fit in this room? Do they like this view? Is the kitchen big enough? These are the types of questions that will assist you in gaining and keeping control.

By asking questions, you will get buyers involved mentally and verbally. Even if they don't respond verbally to a question, they will respond mentally; they will answer it to themselves. "But Mike, if they don't say the answer, how do I maintain control?" By controlling what they think. You're keeping their mind on one thing: whether or not they will purchase the house you're showing them. If you control their thoughts, you certainly control them.

Most of the time buyers will verbally respond to your question. They will also respond with their actions, so you have to watch them—especially their facial expressions. Are they enjoying something about the house? Did your question cause them to smile with contentment, or did they react with a bit of a scowl? These are all answers, so pay attention and you will learn more. You will stay on the right track, and you will keep them on the buying track.

Remember that buyers also will be asking a lot of questions. They don't have to be encouraged to ask them, they just do. You should literally jump for joy when they ask questions, because it shows that they're involved with you and buying mentally. That's what you're working for. The more questions you get, the more you will be in control.

What do you do with a question? You answer it. But don't just stop there. Ask a similar question in return after you've answered their question. This technique is a little difficult at first; however, the faster you master it, the faster you will be earning SIX figures. It's a very powerful technique.

Let's say your buyers are showing all of the buying signals and are excited about the house. They ask, "Does the refrigerator go with the house?" You answer, "I don't know: [keep going] would you like me to include it in the offer?" How simple—from one of their questions, you start to go into a close. It works.

To perfect this "question/question" technique, you need to practice. Start by practicing in your office. Each time someone asks you a question, answer theirs, and then ask a similar question in return. Just a word of warning: Never say, "Why do you ask?" It's just too threatening. The buyer will stop asking questions and cut off a valuable supply of information.

Just a few general examples:

"What kind of car do you drive?"
"A Chrysler. Have you ever driven a Chrysler?"
"How are you?"
"Fine. And you?"
"Can I borrow your MLS book?"
"Sure. Do you have a buyer?"

Do you get the idea? Make it a game and you will learn it faster. I cannot tell you how important this technique will be to your success.

You must know that I believe in questions to keep people involved with what they're doing. Consider this book, for example. How many questions do you think I pose? I really don't know; it must be around 300. Why do you think I do that? To keep you involved with the learning process. I believe the information in this book is so valuable to your success that I try to ensure your interest by asking a lot of questions. Does it work? It does, doesn't it?

You have all heard of the word *synergy,* which means that the total effect of individual parts is greater than the sum. It means that if you take what you have read in this chapter and use it all, it will have a greater bearing upon your success than if you choose to follow only certain instructions. In other words, take everything I've listed under "Making It Easy for the Client To Buy" and use *all* of it *all* the time. Why? Because you want to be a superstar and earn SIX figures instead of just dreaming about it, don't you? This is reality, and it looks good to me.

You know, you've worked hard to get your buyers; they don't just fall out of trees. When you take them out to show them property, you must gain and maintain control of the situation. You can do this by

---

Hi Mike,

I guess I'm one of your newer converts, as we only met a few years ago during one of your seminars in Minneapolis. To be honest, I thought I had a pretty good handle on listing and selling property, but boy, was I in for a surprise! I sat for a day watching you carry on, rant and rave, but most important, try to sell us on a system to increase our production quickly. I guess, more than anything else, I was surprised not only at the ideas but at the fact that I felt they would work.

During the last couple of years, people have told me I'm the number-one female producer in the state of Minnesota. I'm not sure that I am, but I am sure that since I started implementing your simple system and guidelines, my production hasn't done anything but go straight up. You've motivated me not only to list and sell more property, but to place some other demands upon myself that can only make me a stronger and better person. I just want to thank you.

Sandy P.

staying with them and asking questions so that you can learn what they're thinking. If you know what buyers are thinking, you can show them the right property, which will lead to a sale. A sale leads to a commission check and that SIX-figure income of the superstar! Are you ready?

CHAPTER 7

The Listing Presentation

You've been out there prospecting every day, knocking on 100 cold doors until your knuckles begin to bleed. This is your third dry day of negative responses, and you're beginning to doubt what I've told you about cold-call prospecting. Just when you think you should have gone to work for your brother-in-law, a man tells you he would like to list his house. In fact, he has three houses he wants to sell. Can you handle them? Now what do you do? You make an appointment to give your listing presentation.

This chapter covers the following topics:

- Be Ready To List
- The Listing Presentation Defined
- The Listing Presentation

By the time you get to the end of this chapter, you will have a proven one-stop listing presentation.

BE READY TO LIST

"When your ship comes in, don't be waiting at the bus depot."

What does that mean? It means that you need to be mentally ready to list property. How can you possibly be ready to list if your brain keeps saying, "Golf course . . . Golf course . . ."? You can't.

Remember, what are the two basic activities of real estate sales-people? Of superstars? That's right, the listing and selling of property. Did you notice that the word *listing* was one of the two basic activities? So it only makes sense that you should always be ready to list property. By the time you get to the end of this chapter, you will be.

Why is it that you don't list a lot of property? Why aren't you taking ten to 12 listings per month? They're out there; why aren't you getting them? It's because you don't know what to say—and what you do say is not very effective, because you're not meeting the seller's needs. By the time you read this chapter, you will know what to say and do. There will be no more hemming and hawing. There will be more listings, and more listings mean more money. It's going to work like magic.

THE LISTING PRESENTATION DEFINED

A listing presentation is a presentation that qualifies and then solves a seller's problem. You need to know what to do before you can do it, right?

First, the seller must have a problem. "But Mike, all sellers have a problem. They want to sell their house." Well, sort of. The question that you will seek to answer is WHY the seller wants to sell. This is called MOTIVATION.

Without motivation, no matter how great your listing presentation is, the seller isn't going to sell. You have to find the motivation of the seller and be able to judge whether it's strong enough. This is called qualifying. You qualify sellers by finding out why they want to sell. If the seller does not have a definite reason for selling, don't waste your time listing the property.

You need to have a strong listing presentation so you can meet the seller's objections. The objections will always be the same; they just don't change. Most sellers are graduates of good ol' Client University. And guess what? I've got the tapes and all of the course outlines from CU. I'm going to make it very easy for you to meet their objections, because I'm going to give them to you.

What's going to happen if you meet the seller's objections? You're going to be more confident—and if your confidence goes up, you will list more property. Listing more property means more money. This is very sound reasoning.

There are only three major considerations in an effective listing presentation. Know all of the objections a seller is going to have and how to respond to them. Know all of the questions a seller is going to have and the answers. Talk only about things that are important to the seller, and nothing else.

What are the standard objections? You've heard them before. Does "I have a friend in the business" or "We want you to lower your commission" sound familiar? Of course they do, because we've all heard them. You'll find that the listing presentation will answer most objections either directly or indirectly. You're going to love it!

What questions do all sellers ask you? "How much is my house worth?" "How much is going to end up in my pocket?" "How soon are you going to have it sold?" These sound pretty familiar, right? The best thing for you to do is be ready with an answer before the seller asks the question. Once again, the listing presentation will help you do just that.

You know, sellers have only one thing on their mind, and that's the sale of their house. Guess what your conversation should be about? That's right—the sale of their house. Do you have a tendency to talk about other things with sellers? Things like the color of the carpet, a football game or a dog show? Don't talk about things that may be important to you; only talk about the sale of the seller's house. That should be important to you, because when the house sells, you will make money—and not before.

Another way to be ready to give the listing presentation is to test it by having other people evaluate your presentation. There are different ways to do this. For example, you can record one of your presentations on a cassette player. Most sellers won't mind if you have asked them first. Then have your spouse or manager evaluate what you're saying. You can also invite your manager or one of the other agents to go with you on a listing presentation.

Chances are that you will be surprised at what you're actually saying to the sellers. Remember, this is meant to be constructive, and it will assist you in making $100 per hour. Do it and you will have the chance to find out what is good and worth keeping about your presentation. You will also find out what is poor, and you will be able to get rid of that part.

In order to be ready to give your listing presentation, you must have sellers to give it to. How do you find these sellers? By prospecting! Why do so many real estate agents stop prospecting for listings and limit themselves to making less than they could?

Perhaps you don't know how to handle rejection. Once again, it's not directed at you personally but at real estate people in general. Look, if everybody were doing their job to the best of their ability, you would not be facing so much rejection. I sometimes think that you can thank the $10 per hour coffee drinkers for a lot of the rejection that's thrown at you. The secret is not to let it hit you; just say "Fine" and move on to the next house.

I'm sometimes lazy about my work, aren't you? Believe me, we all are. It's a reason we stop prospecting. A close relative of this reason is that you do not set goals for yourself. Goals can be motivators; they can get you out prospecting when you really don't feel like it. Establish some goals to assist you in combating laziness.

I've heard a lot of you say that you prefer being "selling" salespeople. Being a selling salesperson is great, but once you know how, listing is easier. Yes, I know that you get paid faster from a sale than from a listing, and that's a great advantage when you're facing car and mortgage payments. However, have you ever thought about getting the commission for both selling and listing? That's just one of the sweet advantages of listing property; you will make more MONEY.

I also know that the market is so good at times that you don't have to prospect to make money. You must remember that this circumstance is part of a cycle. Even a fool can make money in a good market. What happens when the market turns? Will you be ready to do everything in order to make money? Probably not, so get out there and list. If you know what to do, the market will always be good.

Always be prepared to list. That's what this whole chapter is about—being ready and able to list property. When you come across someone who wants to list property, be ready to take his or her listing. It's really not difficult. If you're on your way to becoming a superstar, you will always be ready to either list or sell property.

"Mike, I've found a seller. Now, what do I do? What do I say?" I'm going to tell you exactly what to say. If you can follow my instructions, you'll be on your way to making more money than you ever dreamed of making. You can bank on it.

THE LISTING PRESENTATION

You're going to love this listing presentation! This is a five-step, one-stop presentation designed to be completed within 45 minutes. Why one stop? Because if you're prospecting, you're going to have too many listings to take. You won't have the time to go back a second time.

"But Mike, my area is different. All the houses are custom built." Okay, your area may be different, but is there any reason you can't get the necessary information over the phone? No, there isn't. You can find out size, style, amenities and builder over the phone. You don't have to make two trips when one is sufficient; your time is too valuable.

There are five steps in the listing presentation. They are:

1. Presenting Yourself
2. The CMA
3. The Net Sheet
4. The Plan of Action
5. The Contract

It's imperative that you keep them in this order. There's a reason I placed them in this order, and you will discover it as you read. Basically, don't mess with something that works well. If it isn't broken, don't fix it.

Presenting yourself is nothing more than establishing yourself as a professional real estate sales agent. You're not there to admire how the home is decorated. What happens if you walk into a house that's a dog? If you're used to commenting upon the decor, what do you say? However, if you haven't made it a habit, then you won't have a problem. Also, you're not a friend they have invited over to play bridge. You're there to list their property for sale—to establish yourself as a real estate professional.

With the Comparative Market Analysis, or CMA, you will be answering the questions that all sellers have. What is my house worth? The sellers will have it on their minds, so you're going to answer it at the beginning.

The Net Sheet is going to tell homeowners how much they're going to walk away with from the sale of their house.

Believe me, once sellers have found out how much their house is worth, they will want to know how much that will mean to their pocket. Base this upon the CMA. This means that you will have filled it out ahead of time. Do not use the amount the sellers think the house might be worth. Why? Because there isn't a seller alive who doesn't think his or her house is worth more than it actually is.

The Plan of Action is where you will be solving the sellers' problem. This is a list of things you will be doing to sell their house. The Plan of Action will handle a lot of objections and begin to close the deal for you.

The contract is the last item. Once you get this signed, you're on your way to a commission check! Isn't that why you're there in the first place?

It's very important that you keep these five steps in the order I've given. You win their confidence. It's logical. It's systematic. It works. You've got to love it.

The importance of trigger cards cannot be overstressed. If you have trigger cards, you won't forget what to say. Are you ever nervous when it comes to a listing presentation? I was. However, with trigger cards I was able to remain on track and to listen to what the sellers had to say so I would know what was important to them. By doing this, I was able to address their concerns.

Do you want to make your own trigger cards? Great. Just take a 5" × 8" index card and print the questions that I give you on them. Yes, print, because it's more legible than writing. The last thing you want to have happen is not to be able to read your own cards. That would really be embarrassing and it would increase your nervousness. Make the printing big and clearly legible, okay?

I was at a sales meeting in New York for a nationwide real estate company several years ago. One of the things the company did was to recognize the top producers of the region. One woman was presented with the top award for both the most listings and the most sales, and it was just her first month in the business. Just so you know, she had 14 signed deals going. If she kept on at that rate, at the end of the year she would have completed 168 deals! I know some people in real estate who don't have 14 deals in a year, much less a month.

You can believe I was interested in why she was so successful, so I took her aside and asked her. She stated that she had been through the company's training program and they had given her scripts of what to say. These scripts were dictated to them during the training session, and she faithfully wrote them down verbatim in her workbook. She took the workbook with her on her appointments for listing and showing property and read directly from it. No fancy flip charts. No trigger cards. Nothing except her workbook.

I asked her if it was difficult using her workbook. She said that it was, but since she didn't know what else to say, it was the only thing she could figure out to do. Amazing.

She wasn't polished in her presentation; she just kept on the track to sell and list homes. She didn't know any better than to do her job. It just shows you the power of a script, doesn't it? How many of you would like 168 deals in a year? Or even 100 deals? How about just 75? Then pay attention and follow instructions.

The first step in the listing presentation is nothing more than asking questions to gain information and establish yourself as a professional.

The script for the trigger card is:

Good evening. I'm (name). May I come in? Yes, write out your own name. You're going to be nervous enough. Forgetting your own name would only make it worse.

Would you mind taking a moment to show me your home? Can we sit at the kitchen table? There are a number of questions I would like to ask. May I ask them now?

1. *Where are you moving to?* This will begin to give you their motivation for moving. If they don't know where they're moving, don't ask question 2, okay?
2. *How soon do you have to be there?*
3. *What do you currently owe on the property?*
4. *How much do you want to list your property for tonight?* It doesn't matter if they're overpriced at this point. You're going to address that in a minute. Just say "Fine," and go on to the next question.
5. *Have you ever considered going FSBO?* Get it out into the open; don't be afraid of it. If they say no, respond with "Fine." If they say yes, you have brought an objection out into the open that you would have gotten later if you hadn't asked. You're ahead of the game. And no, you won't be planting an idea in their brains. If they hadn't thought of it before they spoke to you, they won't consider it now. Trust me.
6. *Are you willing to carry a portion of the financing for the buyer?* Don't get into the facts and figures now. You will do that later. Just say, "Fine."

That's the first trigger card. What have you found out? You have begun to determine if they're motivated or not, and you're beginning to find out what objections you will encounter later.

The next step is to make the CMA trigger card.

1. *Mr. and Mrs. (seller's name), I'd like to ask you again, do you have a specific price that you'd like to list your home for tonight?* I know you've already asked this question. Sometimes the sellers will say, "We don't know. You're the expert, you tell us," to the first question. Quite often when you ask them again, you will find that they did indeed have a price in mind. Usually it's a high price.

2. *There are two parts to a CMA that we must look at tonight. Part 1 we call Fantasy Land; it's what we list houses for. Part 2 we call Reality; it's what we sell them for. Let's go through the two parts together.* What do you do now? You read the CMA to them.

3. *Folks, now that you have seen these prices, and based upon sales it appears that your home should sell for $(price), will you list your home for that price tonight?* This may be the toughest part of the presentation; telling them the truth. Expect some gasps and blustering; that's a common reaction. Also expect something like, "But our home is special. It's worth more." What are you going to say? "Fine."

    If they're willing to list for that price tonight, go directly to step three. If not, continue.

4. *There are three questions I'd like to ask you at this time.*
    *   *Why do you feel your home is worth $(amount overpriced) more than your neighbor's?* Just be quiet and let them tell you. You will hear all kinds of reasons. Remember, just as a buyer buys upon emotion, a seller can be very emotional when selling his house. Your only response should be "Fine."
    *   *If you folks were purchasing a home and two were for sale, one for $(correct price) and one for $(overpriced), which would you probably buy?* You're going to get them here. Most people, using common sense, would buy the less expensive house.
    *   *Don't you think that most people feel just like you?* They're probably going to agree with you, so now you ask them to lower the price. You know what? They probably will.

If they lower the price, go on to step three; if not, continue to question #5.

5. *Mr. (seller's name), if by chance your home has not sold, are you planning to leave your family here until it sells, or take them with you?* If he takes the family and leaves the home vacant, proceed on to question #6.

6. *Mr. (seller's name), how long are you folks in a position to make payments on this property once you've moved and it's vacant?* "We can't do that!" To which you reply, "Fine. Will you lower your price so that it will sell?"

7. *Folks, if you could sell the house tonight, how much would you sell it for?* Generally, it will be for less than the high price that they're trying to stick with.

    "Fine. Would you list it for less tonight?"

    You have to remember that another agent in the office might have a buyer sitting there for this house at the correct price. There's no harm in letting the sellers know this. In fact, it would be a good idea.

    However, if they continue to remain firm on the higher price . . .

8. *We'll list the property for your price, but I want you to understand the property is overpriced. Do you understand what I mean when I say "over-priced"?* Here is where you can make a decision. If the sellers continue to insist upon listing their house at an inflated price, you can decline to take the listing. "But Mike, not take a listing?" That's right, don't take the listing. Why? Because it will take too much of your time, and it will probably turn into an expired listing. Nobody wins in a situation like that. Nobody is happy.

    If you decide not to take the listing say, "Fine. Thank you for your time," and leave. There are too many good listings for you to waste your time on the ones that are overpriced. Also, you're dealing from a position of power. When they see you get up to leave, they will understand that you're serious and might just lower their price. You have taken a giant step toward complete control!

Step three is the Net Sheet. All you have to do is read it to the sellers. Remember that you have filled it out ahead of time based upon the CMA. After you have gone over it with the seller . . .

- *Is this enough money to get you folks to* (place)?
  It's a yes or no answer. If no . . .
- *How much more do you need?*
  Just listen. It's decision time for the seller.

Step four is the Plan of Action. The Plan of Action is shown in Figure 7.1.

This Plan of Action is great! You're going to be doing it all anyway, and now it's down on paper for the sellers to see and marvel at. If you do any combination of the things listed in the Plan of Action on a regular basis, the home will sell. Even if it is overpriced, if you do them all on a regular basis, the home will sell.

When you introduce the sellers to the Plan of Action, emphasize the company objectives. Why? Because these are what the entire office will be doing to get the home sold. The sellers will begin to think that the entire office is working to sell their home, and really, are they wrong? No, you're just putting down on paper what the office would be doing whether or not the Plan of Action existed.

Points 1 through 21 are what you will be doing as an individual to sell the home. This is what *you* are responsible for doing, not the office. You're stating your value to the seller. The list is impressive, isn't it?

The real value of the Plan of Action is as a closing tool. As you read each point to the seller—that's right, you read each point aloud—you can begin to make your closing. Here's how it works:

Read point number one—"Submit your home to the Multiple Listing Service." Then ask the seller, "You do want to be listed in the MLS, don't you?" The seller says, "Yes." What have you just done? You've closed!

Next, read point number three—"Tour your home with my office." Then ask the seller, "Do you want the tour this week or next?" The seller says, "This week." What have you done? You've just closed again.

A great way to use the Plan of Action is to read three points and then close on the next three; then repeat the process. It won't be too long before the seller will get the idea and just say, "Okay, list me." This can be a very powerful tool if used correctly.

What happens if the sellers are willing to list with you, but they want you to cut your commission? Take the Plan of Action and ask them what services they want cut. When they start to point one out, stop them and say, "I'm sorry, that's just too important. Pick another."

FIGURE 7.1   The Plan of Action

Our company objectives are the following:

1. To get as many qualified buyers as possible into your home until it's SOLD.
2. To communicate the results of our activities to you weekly.
3. To assist you in getting the highest possible dollar value for your property with the least number of problems.
4. To constantly look for the best possible methods of exposing your property to potential buyers in the market.

The following is our company's plan for marketing your home:

1. Submit your home to the Multiple Listing Service.
2. Submit copies of your listing to our company's sales staff for their waiting buyers.
3. Tour your home with my office.
4. Promote your home at the real estate board meetings for maximum exposure to the other agents in the area.
5. Develop a list of features and benefits of your home for the cooperating agents to use with their potential buyers.
6. Suggest and advise you as to any changes you might want to make in your property to make it even more marketable to buyers.
7. Constantly update you as to any changes in the market.
8. Knock on 50 doors in the surrounding area.
9. Create additional exposure through a professional sign and lock box.
10. Hold an open house when possible.
11. Advertise when necessary.
12. Prequalify, when possible, all prospective buyers.
13. Make you completely aware of all the various methods of financing that your buyer may want to use.
14. Have the cooperating brokers in the area tour your home.

FIGURE 7.1 The Plan of Action (continued)

15. Provide for the cooperating brokers, on a monthly basis, a list of the features and benefits of your home.
16. Follow up with all of the salespeople who have shown your home for their response.
17. Assist you in arranging interim financing, if necessary.
18. Deliver a copy of your multiple listing and all published advertisements for your approval.
19. Represent you upon the presentation of all contracts by cooperating brokers and help you negotiate the best possible price and terms.
20. Handle follow-up and keep you informed, after the contract has been accepted, on all mortgage, title and other closing procedures.
21. Deliver your check at the closing.

Submitted by: Your Acknowledgment:

_____   _____

Every point in the Plan of Action is too important to cut if they expect you to sell their house. You begin to see its power more and more, don't you?

Do you remember asking them on the first trigger card if they were considering going FSBO? Here's where the answer to that question comes into play. If their answer was no, don't worry about it. If their answer was yes, tell them that all a FSBO can do is to put a sign out, advertise and hold an open house. Why, that's only 3 out of 21 points! Surely they don't want to deprive themselves of the other 18. If they go FSBO, they will not be able to use those other 18 points. You're their key to getting the full service that a professional real estate agent can provide.

Now you're ready for step five, the contract. The sellers are on your side; they have gotten used to saying yes, yes, yes. So you ask them to sign the contract. Chances are that they will continue to say yes, and all you have to do is hand them the pen. Simple! And it works!

Step five has its trigger card:

1. *Fill in the blank spaces on the contract.* This includes the number of bedrooms and bathrooms, pool, square footage, the kind of flooring, etc. Where do you get this information? You get it by asking the seller.
2. *Review the parts you've filled in.*
3. *Review the fine print.*
4. *"Would you sign the contract, please?"*

You've gone through the entire presentation and they want to sign the contract. They're literally begging you for the pen. They aren't going to have any objections because, from the first step through the Plan of Action, you have already handled all of their objections. You're on your way to a commission check.

After the contract is signed:

1. *Suggest any improvements or changes that should be made to the house.* Be tactful! I cannot stress this too strongly. What am I referring to here? Things like cleaning the carpet, moving out some of the furniture if there's too much and cleaning the windows.
2. *"Some salespeople may not show your property. Don't be disappointed."* Why would you say this? If you have listed the property and it's overpriced. This is another opportunity for you to get the seller to lower the price. Take it, if necessary.
3. *"You may hear some derogatory comments about your home because of the price, but don't be disappointed."* Another chance for you to get the seller to lower the price.
4. *"Some offers may come in low, but let's look at all offers carefully."* For the overpriced listing again.
5. *"If you decide to lower your price, will you lower it to $(price) or $(price)?"*
6. *"Would you folks prefer to lower it tonight, or wait two weeks?"* Once again, you're trying to get the sellers to lower the price. What happens if you go through the entire listing presentation and they don't sign? "Fine, thank you for your time."

What else do you do? You take everything with you. You don't leave anything unless you have a signed contract. Nothing is to be left at the house. Not the Plan of Action, not the Net Sheet, not the CMA. "I'm sorry, I can't leave anything with you unless there's a signed contract." It'll work.

This presentation is simple. It keeps you and the buyer on track to the signed contract. It doesn't take long to go through the listing presentation, only about 45 minutes. Realize that with this presentation you're in control. You will make the decision whether or not to take the listing. That's strength and control. Use this presentation and you'll be getting more "good" contracts signed than you ever imagined. Are you ready for a SIX-figure income?

CHAPTER 8

Superstar Methods of Handling Objections

You're faced with objections every day, especially if you're working on becoming a superstar. You're literally surrounded by them. Your children say, "But I did that yesterday." Your husband or wife says, "But honey. . . ." What's the difference between the objections that we are given by friends and family members and those that we get from clients? Money. If we don't know how to handle the objections we get from clients, we might as well wave goodbye to the commission check. If you're becoming a superstar, you will need to know how to handle objections.

This chapter covers the following topics:

- Objection Defined
- First Steps in Handling Objections
- Objections You Will Receive
- Seller's Objections
- Buyer's Objections

Once you understand what objections are and how to handle them, you will make more money. So learn this chapter and become a superstar.

OBJECTION DEFINED

An objection is a question in the mind of the seller that remains unanswered. So what happens when you handle an objection? You're answering a client's question. If a client says, "I want to think it over," he or she really means "If you could tell me more of the benefits of this property, I'll buy from you." Or "I have a friend in the business" means "If you could tell me why your company is better than theirs, I'll list with you."

Did you notice that in both of those comments, clients were seeking more information? That's what handling an objection is all about. What is the result of answering a client's objection? It's right there for you to read: "I'll list with you," or "I'll buy from you." Both of those comments lead to what? More money. It pays to be able to answer their objections skillfully.

There are really two kinds of objections. The first kind are those you will receive from clients; the second kind are those you create before you even start to deal with a client. The second type are the real commission-killers.

How often have you qualified buyers by what they wear or drive, or by their current address? Big mistake—but not an uncommon one; everybody has done it at one time or another. Do you recall my friend who prefers to wear jeans and comfortable shoes when he goes shopping, and who buys with cash exclusively?

How many commissions do you think have been lost because he is not approached by a salesperson most of the time? He conservatively estimates that at least one salesperson a week loses a commission because they don't qualify him.

How many times have you gone to present a buyer's offer and thought, "They probably won't accept this stupid offer"? Of course they won't, if you think like that. How about approaching a FSBO with "They probably won't list with me."

The hardest objections to handle are those in your mind. They are self-defeating. How are you ever going to become a superstar with those kinds of thoughts? It's simple: You're not. Such thoughts become a self-fulfilling prophecy. You destine yourself for failure at a task before you even start.

If you qualify your buyers and sellers and you're in control, there is absolutely no reason you should think those kinds of thoughts. If you don't think you will succeed, don't worry—you won't. On the other hand, if you begin to think and act like a superstar, you'll become a superstar.

There are two kinds of statements a client will make. There are objections, those questions you will need to answer, and there are conditions. Conditions are defined as facts that you can do nothing about. You've got to learn the difference if you're going to be effective.

A client says to you, "I want to buy a $300,000 house. I'll put $3,000 down, and I want a monthly payment of $750." It can't be done. That's a fact and a condition statement.

Another condition statement: "I want to buy a house VA." So you ask, "What years were you in the service?" He responds, "I haven't been in, but I'm thinking of joining." There is nothing you can do for this buyer except point him in the direction of the recruiters. Condition statements are coming right out of Fantasy Land, and there isn't a thing you can do to sell or list this customer, regardless of his or her motivation.

FIRST STEPS IN HANDLING OBJECTIONS

No matter how experienced you are in handling objections, everyone still needs to be reminded of the basics. Why? Because we all have certain tendencies we need to guard against, and we all need to be reminded that if we make certain mistakes, we can kiss our commission checks goodbye.

First of all, do not argue with a customer. I know this is very difficult at times, but you have to remember that the customer is always right. The customer's conclusions, however, may be based upon faulty information. Part of your job is to make sure that the information the customer has is correct.

Why do you think I've given you the word *fine*? It's just so you won't get yourself into trouble. If you argue with the customer, you will lose him. Can you afford to have a commission check walk across the street to another agent? No, you can't, so don't argue. Don't even argue mentally, because what you're thinking will come out of your mouth.

Learn to listen effectively. You were given two ears and one mouth; use them in that ratio. What you need to do when listening to objections is to close off your thinking process and listen; pay attention to what the customer is saying, and then you will be able to answer the objection effectively.

Don't jump to conclusions. You think that you know what the client is thinking, and you interrupt. If you're engaged in listening, this won't happen. That's pretty simple, but I've heard it happen many times. The client says, "I want to——" and the salesperson jumps in with "I know you want to think it over." In reality, the client was going to say, "I want to buy." It happens. We have all heard it—or worse, done it.

Arguing, not listening and jumping to conclusions all arise out of tension. The nearer you get to closing a deal, the more tense you become. You want to get the deal finished. One of the solutions is to close more deals so you won't be as tense when you close. The advantage to this is that you will make more money as you decrease the tension. Sounds good, doesn't it?

We are surrounded by tension in our lives outside of real estate. Tension comes from everywhere: our husbands or wives, our children, finances, in-laws, traffic, our time management. The list is endless. Basically, everything in life causes tension. The only way to eliminate tension is to die. I really can't advise that as a cure.

One way to cope with tension is through exercise. Do you remember that I suggested that you exercise 30 minutes a day? Not only will this get you into better shape and improve your stamina, but it will also reduce the tension you feel.

You're waiting for the perfect house for the buyer. If you wait for the perfect house, you'll have a long wait. There is no such thing as a perfect house. If you ever get a buyer who says you're in the perfect house, close immediately—and I hope that you have a contract with you.

You must answer every objection. It does not have to be a great answer, just an answer. What happens is that you want to overcome every objection. You can't, but you can answer every objection.

Keep your answers simple. "You're right" is a perfectly good answer. Agree with the customers. Who knows, you just might shock them into signing the contract. What are you going to do, argue? I hope not. "I wanted a white house. This is blue." What are you going to say—that it isn't blue? Try, "You're right. But it has everything else you wanted." See how well that works?

Your purpose is to list and sell property, right? Not to memorize complicated answers to the most esoteric of objections. So what should you do? Answer every objection with a simple response.

Question the objection the second time you receive it. Remember the question-question technique? Use it. Answer the objection and then ask a question in return.

Let's say you have a buyer in a house that has a small master bedroom. However, it's right in all other respects: price, down payment, monthly payment and location. The buyer brings up the inadequate size of the master bedroom twice: once in the house, and now as you're filling out the contract. You just agreed with the buyer in the house.

> "The size of the bedroom must be very important to you; this is the second time you've brought it up. If everything else is perfect about the house, would you still buy it?"
>
> "Yes."
>
> "Would you sign the contract?"

If the bedroom is still unacceptable to the buyer, say:

> "Would it be better for you to pay more for a house that had a larger bedroom?"

If the answer is yes, show the buyer another house. If no, ask for the signed contract.

Keep It Simple, Salesperson! We have a tendency to complicate everything. Simplicity always works. Why would you want complex, flashy answers when you won't use the simple, proven answers? Do communications ever get a little tangled in your life, even simple phone messages? Of course they do. Do you see why I tell you to keep it simple? By keeping it simple, you will avoid misunderstandings.

Buyers and sellers aren't as stupid as we would sometimes like to think. If you try to use complicated language that does not answer their question, they will figure it out. Be simple and direct. Don't try to hide behind a flashy response that does not contain substance. All you will do is lose the commission.

There are some things you can do to reduce the number of objections you receive. For example, you can make a better presentation. With a stronger presentation, you will hear fewer objections. Why?

Because you will be answering some questions as you give the presentation.

Also, you can learn to be a stronger closer. A stronger closer will get fewer objections. How do you become a stronger closer? By doing it more often—and the wonderful thing is that you will make more money as you practice. You can start by integrating the closes that I will give you.

You have to understand that the objections never change. It doesn't matter whether you've been in the real estate business for one year or 20, you will hear the same objections.

"I want to think it over."
"I have a friend in the business."
"The price is too high/low."

They just don't change. You would think that agents would be able to come up with answers for them after hearing them so often. Client University hasn't changed this course in 50 years. It's amazing!

OBJECTIONS YOU WILL RECEIVE

You will not like 90 percent of the answers I give you for the objections. That's fine. These are ideas and examples that have been proven successful and are making money for people every day. However, if you want to change or customize them to fit your style, feel free.

One thing these answers all have in common is that they are direct answers that will lead to a signed contract. What happens when a contract is signed? You make more money.

All of the answers start with the words *I understand.* You can substitute the word *fine;* however, if you're using that word a lot, you might want to stay with *I understand.*

Why did I use these words? It shows that you can empathize with clients and it will get their attention. These words will convince clients that you're working for their best interests. And when it comes right down to it, aren't you? If you have qualified them, you have them in a house that they like and can afford. It works!

Several of the answers make a reference to the Plan of Action; you will need to refer back to the Plan on page 113 to answer the objection.

Use the Plan. Why? Because it works! Do you begin to see how my system works together? Sure, you can use one part and it will make you money. But if you use the entire system, you will become a superstar.

SELLER'S OBJECTIONS

"I want to give you only a 30-day listing."

I understand. Many times other salespeople feel that a short listing is a sign of anxiety to sell quickly. Is it your need to sell quickly or the fact that you did not understand all of the items we will be involved in to get your home properly marketed? (Refer back to the Plan of Action)

What other salespeople will see that it's only a 30-day listing? To begin with, the other agents who work in your office. And if your MLS book shows how long a listing is for, all agents in the area will see that it's only a 30-day listing. Plus, you will not be able to effectively do everything in the Plan of Action if you have a short listing. It's as if the seller is tying your hands in your effort to sell his or her house.

"I've never heard of your company."

I understand. Which companies are you familiar with? I think what's important is not so much the name, but the kind of service you'll be receiving. What questions did you have about the services we've discussed? (Refer back to the Plan of Action)

"I'll save the commission by selling it myself."

I understand how you feel. I think that the question you'll be asking is really, "How can we earn the commission?" Let's review again the services that we offer. Will you please stop me when we discuss a point that's unclear to you? (Refer back to the Plan of Action)

"I will list high; I can always come down later."

This is true. However, high-priced listings usually sell other people's homes. Let's review again: How soon do you expect to be moving? How much do you expect to lower the price? When will you want to make your first price reduction—next week or the week after?

"I don't want to sell until I buy."

I understand. Your fear is having your home sell and having nowhere to go, correct? We will work hard now to find you the right home, and we'll coordinate your closing date on your new home so time will not be a problem. Have I explained our swing-loan program?

This is not really a strong objection; this is more a question of motivation. Do they really want to sell? If they do not seem to be fully motivated, take them out and find them a home they like. Then tell them that they cannot have that home until they sell their current home, if that's the case. This can push a slightly motivated seller to become really motivated.

"I must check with my banker [lawyer, etc.]."

I understand. Is it the wording in the contract you want to check on? Should we write the listing/sale subject to your attorney's approval within 24 hours, or would you prefer to go ahead now?

"I want to think it over." (Use the Summary Close)

"I have a friend in the business."

I understand. It's difficult not to deal with friends, but let's take a look at the services that the two companies offer. What you're really concerned with is good service, correct? (Refer back to the Plan of Action)

Here's a little hint: Keep referring back to service. Stress the service you will give the client, and you will get the business.

"Your company is too small [big]."

I understand. It seems what you're concerned with is whether my company can effectively market your home, correct? Let's review the Plan of Action. Please stop me at any part that you don't understand.

"Another company said that they could get me more money."

I understand. Many companies list properties at one price and expect to sell them at a completely different one. That's probably very disappointing to the seller, wouldn't you agree? Let's review our CMA together and again look at the prices, but before we do, could you review with me where you're moving to?

What are you doing here? That's right, you're checking on and reminding them of their motivation for selling. Sellers sometimes need to be reminded of why they are selling their home.

"I don't want to sell my property VA or FHA."

I understand. Would you do me a favor? At least look at all offers, and then together we can make the decision how to sell. You don't want to exclude _____ percent of the potential market, do you?

You need to know how much of your market goes VA or FHA. Remember, in most parts of the United States homes will go one way or the other. If you deal in a market that's too high for these government programs, however, the objection won't arise.

"I don't want a sign on the property."

I understand. May I ask why? Were you aware that a major percentage of our buyers come from our signs? Would you want to exclude _____ percent of your potential buyers?

What do you need to know here? You need to know how many buyers you get from sign calls. Typically, it falls between 25 and 50 percent, although I've heard as high as 80 percent.

"Mike, these answers sound pretty good. But how do I learn them?" There are basically four ways to learn these answers. You can write them down about four or five times with pen and paper; you can use trigger cards; you can practice among yourselves by tossing out objections and giving the answer; or you can try to memorize them. You can also wing it. But why do that when I've given you the answers?

BUYER'S OBJECTIONS

"We don't feel that this is the time to buy."

I understand. There probably is not a "good time" to buy a home. May I ask you what, at this time, is stopping you from making the decision to buy this home?" (Wait for response, then go to the Summary Close)

This is another question of motivation. If you have qualified your buyers, then you will know whether or not they have the necessary motivation to buy. If the buyers do not have the motivation, you may just be wasting your time.

"The area is too new."

I understand. This, of course, gives you a chance to gain much of the appreciation that newer homes experience. Also, a new home gives you the chance to individualize your choice of carpets, landscaping, wallpaper, etc. What changes in this home do you think you will be making after you move in?

"The area is too old."

I understand. The advantage of this area is that you're seeing it at its most developed stage—NOW. There are no surprises. Would you be willing to pay possibly $5,000 to $8,000 more to find the same home in another area that's three to four years newer?

"I don't like the neighborhood."

I understand. Many times we find the home we've always wanted in a neighborhood that's not totally appropriate. In this particular case, are you prepared to pay $5,000 to $8,000 more when we find you the same house in a nicer area?

"The home is too far from the schools."

I understand. Do your children prefer to walk or ride the bus? Fine, let's measure the exact distance to the schools, then decide which is best for them. Are you familiar with the busing system we have here in _____ ?

"The taxes are too high."

I understand. Taxes today are high. What are you paying on your current home? I know you're aware that taxes are deductible on your income tax. Will you be using an impound account or paying your taxes twice a year?

As soon as they answer the question, whether they are using an impound account or paying taxes twice a year, follow it up with, "Fine. Would you sign the contract, please?" This works so well.

"The home is run-down."

I understand. This does offer you the chance to add your own personal touches. Would it be better for you to pay a higher price for a more complete home, or just re-do this one to meet your individual needs?

"The yard is too small."

I understand. What plans do you have for the yard? I know you're aware that this type of yard is easier to maintain and allows you more leisure time. So do you usually take care of the yard yourself, or do you use a gardener?

"The yard is too big."

I understand. This lot is somewhat larger, but remember, a larger lot offers considerably more privacy. What type of plan do you have for your yard?

"The interest rate is too high."

I understand. I'm sure you're aware that your interest is deductible. Also, let's compare the actual dollar cost of the interest that you will be paying versus the interest you thought would be appropriate. What interest rate did you expect to receive?

"The price is too high."

I understand. Prices today are certainly higher than in the past and probably will continue to rise. This, of course, is to your advan-

tage. May I ask how long you think you'll live in this home—five or ten years? (Now reduce to the Ridiculous Close)

"The payments are too high."

I understand, and I agree that payments on most homes are higher today than before. How much did you originally think would be your monthly payment? Let's look at what you like best about this home and see if the additional expense is worthwhile. What did you like best? (Go to "T" Close)

"My uncle [brother, etc.] must see it first."

I understand and I agree that it's important to get your _____ approval. Will they be living with you or making part of the monthly investment? Then there are two ways that we can go: One, we can make this offer contingent upon their approval, or two, we can surprise them and show them that the decision has already been made. Which way should we go?

"We want to think it over."

I understand how you feel. (Now use either the Story Close or the Summary Close)

Do you want to be an effective closer? Do you want to make more money? Practice closing. How do you practice closing? The best way is to show and sell a lot of property. That way you'll be practicing and earning money at the same time. Sounds good, doesn't it?

The better you are at answering objections, the better closer you will become. If you are a stronger closer, you're going to make more money. What does that mean? It means you will be on your way to becoming that $100 per hour real estate superstar.

CHAPTER 9

Closing the Sale

You've got those buyers in the palm of your hand. They are sending you all of the buying signals. You're patting yourself on the back because you had them prequalified with a lender before you showed them property. There's nothing, absolutely nothing, that's going to stand in the way of you getting a commission check. In fact you already have an appointment to look at new cars. "Mike, everything you told me to do works!"

You bring out the contract for the buyers to sign as you're giving them the best sale smile you have. Suddenly they say, "We want to think about it." What? Think about it? "Mike, what do I do now?"

This chapter covers the following topics:

- Closing Defined
- Superstar Closers Are Made
- Closing Techniques

Read on and you will still be able to get that new car.

CLOSING DEFINED

Closing is helping a customer make a decision. Look around. People have a hard time making a decision. If people have a hard time deciding whether they will wear a blue or red tie, or whether they will wear the gray or blue shoes, think about the problem they must have when it comes to the purchase of a house. It must drive some people crazy.

You can save some people's sanity by assisting them in arriving at a conclusion. Sure, you're going to make a commission check after it's all over, but you wouldn't be showing them houses that weren't right for them, would you? Of course not. Remember that you have already gone through a qualifying procedure with them; you know what they want and what they can afford. If you've done everything right, you have them in a house that will meet their need for shelter they can afford. But they are still plagued with indecision. If they are to buy, they need your help.

A woman has been invited to a party. She wants to buy a new dress, so she goes down to her favorite store armed with a charge card that has a zero balance. She can buy whatever she wants. Well, it so happens that this store is having a sale; everything is marked down 60 percent. She goes to the rack and finds a dress she really likes. As she is holding it up in front of a mirror, a salesgirl approaches her and asks if she needs any help. The woman says no. The salesgirl tells the woman that she will be at the cash register if she has any questions.

What do you think happened? The woman left the store without a dress! She had motivation. She had the money. What was the problem? She was not assisted in making a decision to buy. The woman needed to be asked to buy the dress.

Your buyers need to be asked to buy. People expect to be asked to buy, but we don't always ask them. Why not? We think that as a customer we don't like being asked to buy.

If your buyers do not really want to buy a house, why are you showing them property? Certainly it's not for your health. You qualified them and you know they have the money. If you have done everything I've suggested, you're not taking window shoppers out to look at property; you're dealing with motivated buyers that just need a little help in making a decision.

A minister asks people to buy every Sunday. No, I'm not talking about the offering plate. The minister asks people to make a commitment to an idea; a way of life; an intangible. Who do you think has the tougher job: you, selling real estate that's tangible, or the minister who sells an idea, an intangible? Are you kidding me? The minister has a tougher job than you ever thought of having.

A closing is a natural ending to a good presentation. If you have done your job in the beginning by qualifying the buyers and showing them houses that meet their needs and desires, then closing is a natural. You will know when they are in "their" house—they will show all of the buying signals. It will be time to help them make a decision to buy "their" house. It will be time to close the sale.

SUPERSTAR CLOSERS ARE MADE

How can you become a superstar closer? By overcoming your fear of closing. When you conquer your fear of closing, you're going to be closer to earning $100 per hour. Remember, the only activities in real estate that make money are selling and listing. If you can close that sale more often, what will happen? You will make more money!

The first thing you have to do is discover your percentage of closing—how often you have a signed contract when showing people houses.

How do you calculate the figure? Take the last 30-day period; how many people have you taken out to show property, and how many signed contracts did you get? Let's say that you showed four people property and you received one signed contract. That gives you a closing percentage of 25 percent. When I was selling real estate, my closing percentage was 33 percent. That means I closed one out of every three people to whom I showed property. Some people have a closing percentage of 20 percent, while others have one of 50 percent.

It's important to know your closing percentage, because you will then know when to expect a sale. If I had appointments to show property on a Saturday at 10 A.M., 2 P.M. and 4 P.M., I would expect to sell one of the groups on an average day. On a good day, two. On a great day, all three. Knowing when you should sell gives you power, great power.

Let's say that I did not sell either the ten o'clock or the two o'clock appointments; do you know how I would greet the four o'clock appointment? "Good afternoon, folks. I usually close one out of three people to whom I show houses. Guess what? I had two other clients today and they did not buy. You're number three; are you ready to buy a house?" Most of the time they ended up buying.

You have to ask everyone to buy. That's right, everyone. The funny thing about asking people to buy is that sometimes they will say yes. Besides making money, you will increase your closing percentage and become a more powerful closer.

You need to thoroughly understand what closing is in order to remove the fear. How often during our lives are we introduced to new activities that scare us at first?

More often than you think.

Do you remember when you learned how to drive? I do. The instructor took me to one of the busiest freeways in the world on the first day. I was nervous to begin with, but when we got on that freeway I was scared out of my mind. You know what my instructor said to me? He said, "You learn how to drive here and everything else will be a piece of cake." He was right.

We all were a little nervous the first time we were behind the wheel. But with time and practice, that fear was replaced with confidence. The very same thing applies to closing. The more you practice and do it, the less fear it will hold. You will become a confident closer.

You have to learn to control the conversation through questions. There's that word again: control. You're already maintaining control throughout the rest of the transaction process, so why not here? You're qualifying the buyers, you keep them thinking about buying; this is just one more step.

When customers say, "We want to think about it," and you have thoroughly qualified them, what is it that they have to think about? Ask them! Be specific.

"Are you satisfied with the terms?"
"Yes."
"Is the price alright?"
"Yes."
"Can you afford the down payment?"
"Yes."
"Do you like the location?"
"Yes."
"What is there to think about? Sign the contract."

That looks and sounds simple, doesn't it? Believe me, it *is* simple. And it works.

Your fears about closing aren't with you all the time; they are with you only when you begin to see those buying signals. You know the ones I mean: the contented smile, measuring the living room for their furniture, that look of possessiveness. They are literally warming themselves by the hearth. When you see those signals and others like them is when you begin to feel the fear of closing.

When you begin to see those signs, act fast to overcome your fear. What are you really afraid of? There are really only three things that buyers can do: They can reject, accept or embarrass you. That's it. They can reject you by saying no. They can accept you by saying yes and breaking your losing streak. Or they can embarrass you by yelling. So? Remember that great all-around word? It's "Fine." Don't let the buyer intimidate you to inaction.

There's no such thing as a high-pressure salesperson. "But Mike, what about the vacuum, brush, encyclopedia and home-party salesperson?" What about them? It isn't the products they sell, and it's not necessarily the way they go about selling that makes them high-pressure. Then what is it? It's that they don't check the attitude of the person to whom they are trying to sell.

Understand that if buyers are not ready to buy, if they are not showing buying signals, there's nothing you can do to close them. However, if the attitude is right—if they are showing buying signals—then it is not a problem to close the sale, and you will not be perceived as being a high-pressure salesperson.

Can you do anything to affect the attitude of your buyers? Yes. You can keep them thinking about buying by asking questions in the car, by pointing out the benefits and advantages of a particular home; and by taking the time to qualify them before showing them property. What is the word? Control. Control the situation from the beginning.

In order not to fear closing, you must be well-prepared. Superstars know what to say, when to say it and whom to say it to. How do you develop this knowledge? By practice. It's probably not going to happen overnight; it's going to take some time. Do you know what is going to happen as you practice? You're going to have more sales than if you weren't trying to be a superstar. More sales means more money. Believe me, there's a very close correlation between making sales and making money.

Part of being prepared is always having a sales contract with you. No matter how much you think you may control the buyers, you will find that they may want to buy at the oddest times, in the house you least expect them to buy. If you have the contract with you, you can sit right down and fill it out on the spot.

Where is the best place to fill out a contract? That's right—in the house the buyers want to buy. That's the number-one best place. Why? Because they remain emotionally involved with the house. Also, if they have any questions regarding the house, you're in a better place to answer those questions.

Do you remember the buyers that I had to take back to the same house four times before they signed the contract? How many trips would I have made if I had taken the contract with me in the first place? That's right, one.

The only other place to fill out a contract is back in your office. This is definitely a second choice—a distant second choice. The buyers are away from the object of their desire, so they may have a tendency to be a little less emotionally involved. You certainly cannot answer all of the questions about the house that might arise without going back. What happens is that you ultimately lose a little bit of control.

Do it the best way and carry a contract with you at all times. You never know when that buyer might just want to buy a house.

You must be goal-oriented if you're to be a great closer. Set a goal for yourself and strive toward it. Let's say you want to close ten deals this month. You know that your closing percentage is 33 percent. Remember, that means you should close one out of three buyers. Based on that percentage, you know you must show homes to 30 different buyers. Now do you see why knowing your closing percentage is so important? It will assist you as you set goals. You will know exactly what you have to do.

There are several benefits of being a superstar closer. If you have qualified your buyers, you will know they are getting what they want. That will give you a great deal of satisfaction. The company will get what it wants—money. That's right, this is a benefit of being a good closer; the company supports you in what you do, so you want it to stay in business.

And ultimately, as a superstar closer, you get what you want. You get money, satisfaction from a job well done, referrals from satisfied buyers and great peace of mind, because you're helping people achieve their dream of home ownership.

CLOSING TECHNIQUES

I've told you why you've got to be great closers. You do want to make more than $10 per hour, right? Okay, so you've got to become a superstar closer. Now I'm going to tell you how.

There are literally hundreds of closing techniques and variations on them. I'm not going to try to give you all of them. What I'm going to give to you are some very effective closes that will make you money—that will get you closer to that $100 per hour income.

Remember, no single close will work all the time. There's no such thing as a magic bullet close that's always on target. What close you use will be dependent upon what your buyers say. Listen to them and respond accordingly.

The Order Blank Close. The Order Blank Close is defined as asking questions that are easy for the buyer to answer and that cause you to write on the contract. It's easy, and you can't expect a buyer to sign a blank contract. You're faced with the prospect of filling it out. So get the buyers involved with you. Get their help in filling in the blanks on the contract.

Ideally, you will fill out the contract in the home they want to buy. The longer it takes you to get the contract out and begin filling it out, the harder it becomes. So get it out in the house they want to buy. Put it on the coffee table and begin to ask the buyer questions.

Say to the buyer, "May I ask you a few questions?" The buyer will probably react by asking, "Wait a minute. Is that a contract?"

Don't try to hide the fact that it's a contract. The buyer is not stupid. "Yes, it is. Let me write down some of the facts and figures so you can make a decision." What are you telling the buyer? That you want to help him or her make the best decision possible. You're maintaining control without being pushy.

Okay, now for the questions:

1. *Is today's date_____ or _____?*

Name today's date and the next date. Get the buyers involved from the very beginning. Let them help you, or think that they are helping you. What you're doing is beginning to exert your control.

2. *Regarding personal property, the sellers have offered to leave _____ and _____. Do you want anything else?*

The key words here are "regarding personal property." This is what the buyers want the sellers to leave when they move.

3. *Regarding deposit . . .*

You're going to name the price and state that the customary deposit is $_____. Then give the buyers a choice between deposit amounts. They will choose the lowest price or make a counteroffer. Accept it. You're going to get the buyers more and more involved with the buying process.

4. *Do you want to close in 30 or 45 days?*
5. *Would you like to check appliances?*
6. *Do you want to schedule the walk-through two or three days before the house closes?*

What do all of these questions have in common? They all lead to something being written on the contract. You've involved the buyers in supplying you with information that will lead to the contract being completed without your losing control. It works very well.

When it comes to the purchase price, do not ask the buyers how much they want to offer. Why? They will always offer less than the asking price. If the price is close to fair market value, insist on the full price. Why? Because you can assume that the buyers are serious about wanting to buy the house.

If the buyers want to offer less and are emphatic about it, say, "Gosh, I thought you wanted to buy this house." If they still don't want to offer full price, you can do one of two things: Either take out a CMA and show the buyers that the house is fairly priced, or offer to show the buyers houses that may be more in the price range they want to offer.

On the other hand, if the house is priced over the fair market value, you can use the CMA to help the buyers determine what the house is worth.

Remember, if you spend more time qualifying buyers, you will spend less time closing. Time spent at the front of a deal, before you ever show them property, will be saved when you find them the right house. You will be sure of the house they want and how much they are willing to pay.

The Signature Close.   There's no definition for the Signature Close. The only requirement is that this close follow the Order Blank Close. I mean, you wouldn't ask a buyer to sign a blank contract, would you? Of course not.

To set up this close, say, "Let's first review what we've written," and quickly review the contract. Then say, "Let's review the fine print involved." This is an overview, not a line-by-line review.

Now, for the close. It's so easy.

Say to the buyer, "Would you sign the contract, please?" The buyer has been involved in filling out the contract; you've agreed on the price, you've reviewed the entire contract, you're in complete control, so ask for the signature.

This must be the toughest question real estate salespeople ask. Why? Because it's just not asked that often. So get used to it and start asking. What do you think will happen? You'll start making more money.

The Story Close.   The Story Close is telling the buyer a story about another buyer who had the exact same problem, and how you solved his or her problem. There are some special requirements with this close.

First, the story must be true. Don't make it up as you go. Why? You might be caught and lose the entire sale. True stories are always a little more entertaining and can be told with a sincerity that you might not otherwise have.

Second, never tell a story about yourself. Why? Because the buyer is going to have a little trouble believing it, even if it is true. Why risk the trust you have established at this point when you're so close to that commission check?

There's a story that I used about a couple in Huntington Beach, Calif., when I was selling real estate. Jim and Linda were in love with a house that met all their needs. They had all the buying signals. So what was the problem? The house was fairly priced at $31,500, and the price they wanted to pay was $30,000. Jim and Linda ended up signing the contract for $31,500. After living in the house for five years, Jim and Linda sold the house for $135,000.

What basic emotion does this story appeal to? Greed. Is that a strong emotion in most people? Yes, it is. Is it a true story? Yes. Do I make myself out to be the hero of the story? Well, sort of . . . Okay, I'm the hero, but I never come right out and state it. Jim and Linda closed more deals for me than they will ever know.

The "T" Close.   This closing technique is also known as the "Ben Franklin Technique."

This close is very effective when the buyers do not have specific objections but still seem indecisive. Remember, closing is nothing more than helping buyers arrive at a decision. This decision will result in a commission check for you if you have done your job by qualifying your buyers.

What you need to do is to turn the contract over, or have another piece of paper handy, and draw a line down the middle and one across the top. On one side of the line, write reasons the buyers should buy the property; on the other side, write reasons the buyers give not to buy the property. The trick is to always make sure that the "reasons to buy" side is longer than the "reasons not to buy" side. How do you do that?

What you will need are some stock reasons to buy that apply to all houses in the area. A list of benefits might include things like proximity to churches, schools and shopping; no traffic; close to freeways; and close to recreation. You want to overwhelm the buyers with benefits to the point that they feel it would be a great mistake if they did not buy. And miracle of miracles—if done correctly, a commission check will arrive in your pocket. What could be better?

Reduce to the Ridiculous Close.   In the "Reduce to the Ridiculous Close," you're breaking the objection down to the smallest part, and then calling for a decision. You must memorize this close. Believe me, you will see why. The buyers really want to buy the house, but they think the price is just too high. Start with:

1. *It appears that there are only three reasons you would not buy this house today. Down payment, interest payments and purchase price.* You're going to get them to agree with you, which is good.
2. *Do you have the down payment?* You know they do if you have qualified your buyers. They may just need to be reminded.
3. *Can you change the interest rates?* The obvious answer they will give you is "No." Okay, so what is their problem? It's the price!

4. *John and Mary, if you could buy this house today for $10,000 less, would you?* They will probably answer "Yes."
5. *How long do you think you will live in this home—five or ten years?* No matter what they say, settle on ten years; it's easier on the math.
6. *Let's say ten years. If you stayed in this home for ten years, it would only cost you an additional $1,000 per year.*
7. *Do you take a two-week vacation every year?* They will probably answer "Yes."
8. *Then you're actually in the house 50 weeks a year. This house would only cost you an additional $20 per week.*
9. *How many days a week will you actually enjoy this house?* They will answer that they will enjoy it every day of the week.

Do you see what you're doing? You're continuing to keep them thinking about buying. You're controlling the situation by asking questions. These questions are continually heading toward the smallest portion—the lowest common denominator.

10. *Do you realize that this house will cost you $2.85 per day to enjoy?*
11. *For $2.85, you can't afford not to purchase this home. Will you sign the contract?*

Folks, once again, you must memorize this close. Think how embarrassed you would feel if you started this close and did not have command of the figures, or if you constantly needed to refer to a calculator. It would just not have the same effect.

Also, did you notice the last question—"Will you sign the contract?" You need to ask that question. You will be surprised at how much your percentage of closing will increase if you just ask that one question more often. Do you know what else will increase? Your income!

The Summary Close.   The Summary Close is a method of summarizing the various objections that a buyer will give you and then pinpointing the most specific one. This close is particularly effective with the dreaded "I want to think about it."

When buyers say that, they are telling you absolutely nothing, so you need to find out what they are thinking. How are you going to do that? By asking questions—simple questions that the buyer can answer with a yes or a no.

"We really appreciate what you've done today. You have been the best real estate agent so far. You have shown us a wonderful home, but we want to think about it."

"I can really appreciate that. Will you promise to think about it tonight?"

"We certainly will."

At this point, you can almost see a sigh of relief. The buyers have not had to make a decision yet. If all goes well, they will not have to decide anything. They think that they are in control.

"Can I ask you a couple of questions before you go?"

"Sure."

"You liked the price. Is the price one of the things you want to think about?"

"No."

"Monthly payment?"

"No."

"Size of home?"

"No."

"Area for the children?"

"No, that's fine."

"Location?"

"No."

"Decorating?"

"No."

"Well, there doesn't appear to be anything for you to think about. Will you sign the contract?"

What are you trying to find out with this close? You want to find out if the buyers have a specific objection to the home. If they do, then you can go back and address yourself to that issue. If there really isn't an issue and the home is right for the buyers, then you need to help them make a decision, which you just did.

You see, these closes are predicated upon you doing the work at the front end of the deal by qualifying your buyers so that you know they're motivated and have the money to buy. Once you know that, your position becomes stronger and more secure. You gain the control.

You know when to help the buyers make a decision—when to close the sale.

What does this mean to you? It means more money in the form of commission checks. It means that you're on your way to becoming a superstar—to earning that $100 per hour. Are you beginning to see how my system is organized, and that each part builds upon the other until you get the sale in the most efficient manner? Of course you do. And the clearer it becomes to you, the more money you will make—and the closer you are to becoming a superstar. Are you ready?

CHAPTER 10

A System for Presenting Offers

How hard have you worked to get this far? How many hours have you spent prospecting, qualifying, previewing and showing property? How many people have you talked to just to get an offer? The bottom line is that you have a lot invested in the offer, so doesn't it make sense to make the best presentation possible? This chapter is going to tell you how to do it.

This chapter covers the following topics:

- Don't Lose It During the Presentation
- Getting More Offers Accepted
- The Presentation

Read, learn and apply what I give you in this chapter, and you can't help but earn more money.

DON'T LOSE IT DURING THE PRESENTATION

More sales are lost at the presentation than at any other time during the deal. Now you *do* have something to lose. Before, when you did not have a signed contract, you really didn't have anything; there was no promise of a commission check. But now you have a signed contract; an offer to buy a house; the promise of a commission check if you can just get the seller to accept the offer. You're beginning to get a little excited. But don't spend the commission check just yet.

Remember, just because you have an offer to present doesn't mean that it's going to be accepted. There's still plenty of time to mess it up if you aren't careful. So what are you going to do to ensure at least a fighting chance of having the offer accepted? The best thing to do is to know why a deal might fall apart once the offer is made.

You now have an organized presentation for all aspects of the sale, except presenting the offer. Does that make sense? No, it doesn't, because getting the offer accepted is crucial to you making a commission check.

One reason the offer may not be accepted is that you're not prepared to answer the seller's objections. Sellers are only going to have two objections about offers: One, they're going to want more money, and two, they want a faster sale. "But Mike, I already knew that. How do I answer those objections?" It's all in the presentation; how you present the offer and what you emphasize. I'll show you what I mean a little later.

Another reason the sale might be lost is that we forget that selling a home is as emotional for the seller as buying is for the buyer. What kind of memories do you have wrapped up in your home? A lot of pleasant memories. Don't forget that the seller has the same kind of memories.

One of the things I did when a home sold was to take the picture of the sellers putting out a SOLD sign. Normally, this was a very happy time for most families. Alex, whose home I sold for full price, was crying as he held the sign. I was a little surprised.

"Alex, what is wrong?"

"You sold the home today that I raised my children in."

Do you think Alex had some fond memories? Of course he did. Realize that some sellers will have memories that are just as strong. Selling their home may be a bittersweet experience; they may know that it's the right decision, but it's a very difficult time.

How do you compensate for the sellers' emotional attachment to their home? You create a sense of urgency for the sellers and yourself. If the sellers remain emotional, it's easy for them to get off the track.

You want to keep them from sitting on the offer for days, which they will do.

How do you do this? By writing into your offer that the seller must respond within a set time. What is the right amount of time? I think that somewhere between six and ten hours of the time you write the offer is equitable. This will give you time to present the offer and the seller a little time to think about it. Please note, "a little time."

Why only six to ten hours? Remember, I said you had to create a sense of urgency for yourself? There's nothing like a deadline to create a sense of urgency. This means that you have to get in and present the offer quickly, and you will get a quick response. The quicker you know, the better it is for you and your client.

Don't be afraid to limit the time that the seller has to accept or reject the offer. Why? Because you're establishing control. There's that word again. I cannot overemphasize the importance of gaining and maintaining control. If you tell a seller that he or she has to respond by a certain time, who has control? You do. If you have control, if you're creating the sense of urgency, who wins? You do. Winning comes in the form of a commission check.

GETTING MORE OFFERS ACCEPTED

You do want that commission check, right? What you need to do in order to get more of them is to increase your percentage of offers accepted. You want to get more sellers to say yes to your offers than say no. Ultimately, you're working toward 100 percent of your offers being accepted. You may not achieve that goal, but you need to keep striving in that direction.

Just as you have calculated your closing percentage, you should calculate your percentage of offers accepted. You have to determine how many offers you have presented and how many were accepted in the last 30 days; then calculate the ratio for your percentage.

Why do you want to do this? It's to help you set your goals. If you're having only 25 percent of your offers accepted, you know that you need to do some work on your presentation, providing the offers were good. If you want to become that $100 per hour real estate agent, you have to continually improve your skills.

Remember, you must create and maintain a sense of urgency for the seller and yourself. You must begin to gain some control.

You need to work hard to get as close to full price as possible. The closer you get to full price, the more motivated the seller will be. If the seller is motivated, the sense of urgency is easier to maintain.

Now, this only makes sense if the property is not dramatically overpriced. If it is overpriced, you have a responsibility to inform your buyers and let them make the decision as to how much they want to pay. If, on the other hand, the property is at fair market value, don't even ask the buyers what they want to offer. Assume that they really want the house and will pay full price.

You need to get as much credit information on the buyers as possible before you present the offer. This will be very simple if you had them prequalified with a lender before showing them property. This will place you in a much stronger position.

"Mr. and Mrs. Seller, let me tell you about my buyer. He has worked at the ABC Company for 23 years, where he is currently employed as a manager in manufacturing. The offer includes a down payment of $35,000, the balance to a new loan. The good news is that they have already qualified for a loan."

Do you think having this kind of information in the presentation will put you in a stronger position? Of course it will. Do you see why it is so important to qualify all buyers before showing them property? It makes it so much easier at the end, doesn't it? Can't you just see the sellers counting the money from the sale when you give them this kind of information?

Another thing you need to do is to get the largest deposit from the buyer as possible. This is going to show the seller that your buyer is serious. It also works on the greed of the seller. How often do your sellers hold in their hands checks made out to them for 5, 10 or 20 thousand dollars? That's a powerful tool.

"But Mike, how do you get these large deposits?" I have a new and revolutionary way of getting large deposits—ask for them! The perfect deposit would be the full purchase price, right? But how often do we see that? Not often, so we go to the next best thing, which is the full down payment.

"But Mike, what if they don't have the full down payment?" Then you can make it a progressive deposit. What's that? It's where the buyer gives you a deposit for the house now, and every couple of weeks adds to the deposit. I would write it into the contract, because it will look good to the seller. This progressive deposit shows the seller that the buyer is serious about buying the house.

Large deposits can make a difference to buyers as well; it is a good gauge of how serious they are about buying a house. I was called in as a consultant by a company that was writing 100 deals a month, but 50 were falling out. Why? Most of their deals were going VA no/no—VA buyers with no closing costs and no down payment, with a $50 deposit. The first day I was there, a new company policy was instituted: No deposits of less than $500 were to be accepted. What happened? Their business was off by 20 percent in the first 30 days; they were only writing 80 deals instead of 100. But only 7 percent were falling apart. That means that 74 deals were going through! That's a 50 percent increase in just 30 days!

Why? Because they started taking larger deposits from the buyers. Do you see why large deposits are so important? Not only are they good when you present the offer, but the buyer also feels more committed to the purchase. And if the buyer feels committed, the deal has a much better chance of being completed.

Another thing you need to do is complete a Net Sheet based upon the offer, even if it's full price. "But Mike, I'm the selling agent, not the listing agent." I know that. However, you do want to sell the house, don't you? Don't assume that the listing agent has filled out a Net Sheet. If you fill one out, you will never be without one. Besides, it will work as part of your presentation; it will put you in a stronger position. The buyer will know exactly what he or she is going to end up with.

If you're going to be selling another agent's listings, you will need to get his or her cooperation; work for it. I realize that most of the time offers are given over the phone. This is not the best method. The best method is to make the offer in person. That way you can see reactions and read body language. You're also assured of having the seller's full attention. It's a plain and simple fact that you will get more offers accepted if you present them in person than if you do it over the phone.

Prior to going to the house to present your offer, meet with the other agent. No, this is not so you can team up against the seller. If you meet with the other agent, you can explain the offer. This will work for you and you can gain cooperation. Perhaps the other agent even knows something that can help you as you make the presentation.

I know that offers are sometimes given at the listing agent's convenience. This means that they may be given immediately or in two days. Now do you see why it's important to write an acceptance deadline into the contract? It gives you a stronger position from which to deal with the listing agent.

Wouldn't you react a little quicker if you heard, "My buyer wants an answer from your seller six hours from now. Otherwise, the offer is null and void." If it's a bona fide offer, the listing agent has a responsibility to get it to the seller in a timely fashion if at all possible. Does this put you in a stronger position? Of course it does. This approach gives everybody a sense of urgency that they might not otherwise have. It works.

Try to discern the seller's motivation before you go to the house by asking the listing agent. Chances are the agent won't know, but ask anyway. "Where is your client moving to? When does your client have to be there?" These questions are right off your qualifying sheet. If the agent does not know, ask those questions first when you start talking with the seller.

If you're sitting there with an offer in hand, the question is, who is going to present the offer? In presenting an offer, there's only one objective: to get the seller to accept the buyer's offer. That way, you make a commission check. That's the goal, isn't it?

Again, always offer to meet with the listing agent prior to presenting the offer. If the listing agent will not meet with you, you present the offer. When you arrive at the house to present your offer and the listing agent asks to see a copy of the offer, refuse. Firmly state that you think it is best if you present the offer in its entirety and answer questions from everyone afterward. Then present your offer.

The purpose of a prior meeting with the listing agent is so he or she will have a clear and concise idea of what the offer is and how it will work for the seller. Believe me, it's to everybody's advantage if you meet with the other agent prior to presenting your offer. You will be in a much stronger position if you have the agent's cooperation.

You can also find out what the seller's motivation is if the listing agent knows, and if the offer might be accepted. Most of all, you can gain the other agent's cooperation and get him or her on your side prior to presenting the offer.

If you're able to meet with the other agent prior to presenting the offer and the agent becomes very negative, you will need to present the offer. Make it easy for the listing agent to "let" you present the offer. Say that you're willing to let the seller get mad at you; that it's important for the seller to continue to have good relations with the listing agent; and that you're willing to help him or her get off the hook.

Now, if the listing agent will not allow you to make the offer and it's a bona fide one that the seller deserves to see, you can go to his or her boss. If the boss stands behind the agent, you can go to the real estate board. If the real estate board is unavailable, you can go directly to the seller after going to your broker. I've had to follow the above trail of authority in just a couple of instances in all my years in real estate. *This is a last resort option.* Make sure your buyers are serious and that the other agent understands this before you start going up the line. Believe me, you will be stepping on a lot of toes as you go, but as long as you follow that trail, you will be doing nothing unethical or illegal.

Just a word about your relationship to buyers and sellers: Think of them as *the* buyer and *the* seller. Too often you may think in terms of *my* buyer and *my* seller; you get very possessive. When you begin to think like that, you begin to think for them rather than letting them make their own decisions. Let them decide whether or not to accept an offer. You might advise them, but that's all.

If the listing agent becomes excited about the offer, let him or her make the presentation. This only makes sense, especially with a strong agent, who will know the sellers better than you do. Because of that, he or she might be able to do a better job presenting the offer than you could.

THE PRESENTATION

Okay—for whatever reason, you're going to present the offer. Like everything else, there's a successful way to do this that will result in more signed contracts. If you want to be a superstar making $100 per hour, follow my instructions.

The first step is to determine the seller's motivation. If nothing else, ask the seller, "Where are you moving?" and "How soon do you have to be there?" If you already know, you can say, "I'm aware that. . . ." Okay? This brings it right out in the open from the beginning.

Next, discuss the qualifications of your buyers. Who they are, where they work. If you have done so, tell the sellers that the buyers have been financially prequalified. This is the time to go over the credit application. Let the sellers know who wants to buy their house. Remember, it's an emotional time for the sellers.

On to the deposit. Literally wave that deposit check under the noses of the sellers. Let them see and touch it. Be careful what you say! Know whether or not the deposit is refundable. Don't tell the buyers that it is theirs to keep if you don't know or you aren't sure. By not knowing, you could get yourself into a lot of trouble. My advice is to know.

Now read the contract from the bottom. Why? Because if the offer is for less than full price, you will come to it last. However, if it's a full-price offer, read it first.

As you read the contract, use common sense—read only those parts you have filled in. Mention the benefits to the sellers: down payment and deposit. Remember, let them hold on to the deposit check, especially if it's a large deposit.

I have suggested that you fill out a Net Sheet, and you should have done so. Show the Net Sheet to the sellers. Further discuss the advantages to the sellers, like how much they will net.

Review the benefits of the offer to the sellers. If applicable, bring up things like a quick closing; that there are no contingencies; and mention that large deposit.

The next question is very important to your success. "Would you sign the contract, please?" You're going to be surprised how many non-full-price offers will be accepted if the sellers understand how they will benefit and are asked to sign the contract.

If the other agent asks you to leave the room at this point, it's clear that he or she wants to discuss the offer with the sellers. Try not to have to leave the room. Ask the sellers directly, "Do you have any questions about the offer?"

If they do, who could better answer those questions than you? Certainly not the other agent. Who is better to answer any questions about the buyers than you? Nobody! Again, don't be afraid to ask the sellers to sign the contract.

If you're the listing agent, cooperate with the subagent. Offer to meet prior to an offer being presented to the seller. If it's a good offer and the subagent is excited about it and is a strong agent, let him or her make the offer. If it's a bad offer and you have met with the selling agent in advance, let him or her make the offer. If you can help the subagent make the offer or can legally give information that would help his or her presentation, do so. Your cooperation will be gratefully accepted.

Now, if the subagent will not meet with you under any circumstances prior to presenting the offer, take and maintain control. How? By taking him or her through the offer presentation process via asking questions. Ask the sellers to tell the other agent their motivation for selling. Ask to see the deposit. Ask about the buyers. Just take the other agent through the entire presentation from the other side. You will definitely maintain control of the situation and, who knows, may actually be helping the other agent.

You may be involved in a multiple-offer situation. I have some special rules about these. If you're a subagent, you want all offers to go together. This means that you all hear one another's offers. The key is for you to go last; this way, you can hear all the other offers and can perhaps tailor your presentation accordingly.

"But Mike, how do I make sure that I go last?" Ask the others to go first. Ask them when their offers were written and have the earliest time go first, and so on, regardless of what time your offer was written. You want to gain some control in this situation. So when "Who wants to go first?" is asked, take control and ask about the relative times of the offers. Just respond with, "You get to go first. You second. I guess I'm last."

If, on the other hand, you're the listing agent, you want all of the offers separately. Have the other agents wait in different rooms as a presentation is being made.

You want the control, remember?

When a seller receives a telephone offer, you want to be on an extension to hear what is being said. After the offer, make the seller send a fax or telegram to the other agent either accepting, rejecting or counteroffering the offer. This will keep everything clear in everybody's mind. There will not be any confusion.

I cannot possibly cover everything that could happen when you present an offer. The best thing to do is follow the presentation and use common sense. There's no substitute for good common sense when you're faced with an unusual circumstance.

Remember the word *delegation* from the chapter on time management? Here is where it fits in. When you get a signature on a contract, you should inform the buyers/sellers that if they have questions regarding the closing process, they can call the closing officer, title officer, mortgage banker, etc. This will save you a lot of headaches and allow you to go out and make another deal, or two, or ten while this one goes through the process of closing.

Once again, I cannot possibly cover all situations that might arise. The most important thing is to use common sense. Try to gain and maintain control of the situation. Create a sense of urgency for all parties concerned; this will help you gain control. Ask a lot of questions and wait for the answers. Don't forget to listen to those answers.

If you follow the offer presentation that I've given you, you will close more deals. You will become a superstar. More deals means more money. Doesn't that mean that you're getting closer to your goals and dreams?

Hi Mike,

I've been told time and time again that I started in real estate at the wrong time—right in the middle of 1980, the heart of a real estate recession. Of course, the advantage I had was that I didn't know it couldn't be done or that the market was that bad, because I had nothing to compare it to. By my third year I was closing over $5 million but felt that I had peaked.

In early 1983, I signed up to take one of your Action Workshops. You asked me why, with my production, I was taking your program. My answer was simple: I wanted to go to $10 million in the next 12 months. Both my associate and I have virtually spent all of our time reading, listening to cassettes and attending seminars, not only trying to find ways to improve ourselves personally, but also to improve our production. Believe me, there is no better system than the one you keep sharing. It works for everybody every time, as long as the agents are willing to go out and work the system.

I only wish that I had gone through your Action Workshop in 1980 rather than 1983. My production would have gone a little higher and a little faster.

Thanks, Mike.

Dody D.

CHAPTER 11

How To Make Superstar Selling Work for You

I've given you a proven, systematic plan for your success. You have learned about all aspects of a transaction, from prospecting to presenting offers to closing the sale. This chapter will show you how to put it all together.

Let's get one thing straight before I tell you the plan. You must play the numbers game; you don't have a choice if you're going to be a superstar. Remember, studies show that for every 100 people you contact, one person will either buy or sell real estate. You get one deal for every 100 people that you talk to when you cold call in person.

Wouldn't it be great if those people who wanted to buy or sell real estate were required to wear a sign? That way you could find them without any problem. Knowing you're going to get one deal when you talk to 100 people isn't quite as good, but at least you'll know when you're getting close. If you're talking to number 73 and you don't have a deal, you know that somewhere among the next 27 people a deal is probably lurking. You just have to go and find it.

When I first started speaking, I had a few contacts, but not many. I knew that if I were going to be a success in this business, I was going to have to play the numbers game. So what did I do? I sat on the edge of my bed and made 50 phone calls a day, using a script, five days a week for two years. Please note that I did not have an office from which to transact business; I did it all from my bedroom. It worked.

I am going to give you two plans. You choose which one you want to follow. It doesn't matter which plan you select; the chances are your income will soar if you just follow one.

I need to tell you about the basis for the income figures that I will give you. First of all, I've used the national average of one deal in 100 people; that's 100 contacts you must make. If you don't make contact with a responsible party like an adult, the call or door does not count. Also, because it's an easy figure to calculate, I used an average sales price of $100,000. That kind of sale, based upon a 6 percent commission with a 50/50 split, would give you a commission check of $1,500, right? If your commission is higher, great—You'll make even more money!

Also, I did not figure in any double commissions, which you get when you sell your own listings. Why? Because I couldn't even begin to figure out an average number. Remember the policy on showing property: Show your own listings first, followed by company listings, followed by other brokers' listings. By doing this, you're bound to sell more of your own listings and make more money.

Okay, on to the plans.

MIKE FERRY'S 30-DAY SUPERSTAR PLAN

1. Knock on ten cold doors a day, five days a week, for four weeks. If they aren't at home, or you don't talk to an adult or responsible party, they don't count.
2. Make ten cold phone calls a day, five days a week, for four weeks. Use the same rule as above: If they aren't at home, they don't count. You must speak to an adult or responsible party.
3. Talk to two FSBOs a week for four weeks. They must be at home. Just driving by the home and imagining yourself talking

to them doesn't count. You must stop the car and go to the door. Do not use the telephone; it's not as effective.

4. Contact two expired listings a week for four weeks. Again, you must talk to them in person. Do not use the phone either to talk to them or to attempt to set up an appointment.

5. Preview five other brokers' listings five days a week for four weeks. This is not your company caravan; you still must go on that.

6. Hold two public open houses during the four weeks with lots of flags and signs. (If you do steps one through five, you don't have to do step six.)

If you faithfully follow steps one through five, you will talk to 524 prospects in 30 days. That means you will probably have at least five deals going in 30 days. Average commission of $1,500 each gives you a monthly income of $7,500, which means $90,000 per year at the very least. Remember, this does not include any double-commission deals. Seven of those would boost you over $100,000 per year!

I want to be sure you understand something. Steps one through five were based on doing an activity *five* days a week—not seven. Take two days a week off. This is not an option! Fill out your time planner so that you can accomplish steps one through five in the five days that you work.

Do you see the beauty of this plan? Just take the skills I've given you in this book, and you're on your way to a superstar income. There won't be anything that will get in your way as you go for $100,000. You have no idea how excited you'll be as you begin achieving your goal, and you'll begin to see results within 30 days. You won't even have time to get discouraged.

"But Mike, what if I only get four deals?" Try it again next month. You may get six or eight deals. Remember, one deal in 100 is a national average; it happens to be an accurate average that has been borne out all over the United States—but an average nonetheless. If you get four deals one month, chances are you will get six deals the next.

Also, if some of the techniques I've given you are new to you, you will need to practice. So the first month may be a little low. However, time and time again, new licensees using my techniques are holding to the national average of one deal in 100 people.

MIKE FERRY'S 90-DAY SUPERSTAR PLAN

1. Knock on 20 cold doors a day, five days a week, for 12 weeks. If you don't talk to an adult or responsible party, the door doesn't count.
2. Make 20 cold phone calls a day, five days a week, for 12 weeks. You must talk to an adult or responsible party, otherwise the call doesn't count.
3. Talk to five FSBOs a week for 12 weeks. Again, this must be done in person, not on the phone. Don't forget to stop the car; just thinking about talking to them doesn't count.
4. Talk to five expired listings a week for 12 weeks. Don't call first. The same rules apply here as in step three.
5. Preview five other brokers' listings a day, five days a week, for 12 weeks. Two or three of these should be tenant-occupied. Those tenants will make for good prospects; you know they will have to move and that they like living in a house.
6. Hold one good open house a week for 12 weeks. Use a lot of signs and flags. (If you do steps one through five, you don't have to do step six.)

If you follow steps one through five faithfully, you will talk to 2,864 prospects in 90 days. How many deals should you get? How does 29 sound? Sounds good to me.

Based upon a commission check of $1,500, 29 deals should give you a quarterly income of—are you ready for this?—$43,500. I have to say that again. That's a quarterly income of $43,500! That works out to $174,000 per year. Not too shabby!

The next and last plan is my Six-Month Plan. If you are just getting started in the business or have been in it for a short while, this plan is not for you. However, if you are an experienced real estate sales agent who wants to become a top producer and really begin to earn that SIX-figure income consistently, then this is your plan. You will be making more money than you thought possible.

MIKE FERRY'S SIX-MONTH SUPERSTAR PLAN

1. Establish a 300- to 400-person people farm and send a mailing every 45 days.
2. Develop a specialty, such as expired listings or FSBOs, and contact eight per week.
3. Call 25 people per week from your people farm and ask for referrals.
4. Develop an interoffice referral program with five agents. Use only good agents.
5. Preview ten other brokers' listings per week. Out of these ten, five should be tenant-occupied.
6. Do two listing presentations and two showing appointments per week.

What does it take? It takes sticking to a plan. So what is stopping you from becoming a superstar and making superstar money? Nothing.

Take out your daily time planner and fill it out according to how much you want to make. That's right, just block out the time you will need for each activity, and start doing it today. Do not wait for tomorrow. If you wait for tomorrow, you will never start.

Too often, success in business costs you success in your personal life. That does not have to be true. Your happiness should be measured not only by your net worth, but by the happiness of those around you: your family.

Some of the same principles that will make you successful in real estate have direct application to your personal life—like persistence and creativity. Life with another person or persons is not always easy; this is where persistence pays off. Because, while it may not be easy, its value is astronomical. Make persistence a part of your family life; persistently love your family.

Creativity also has some direct applications. When you're discouraged from prospecting, do you just give up and go home? Not if you're going to be a superstar! What do you do? You find a new way or change an old way. That's called creativity.

Do the same thing at home. Whether your family is one other person or ten other people, find something new to do with them on a regular basis. Or do an old activity in a new way. Use your imagination. Be a superstar at home, as well as in the office.

At a recent seminar, I asked 50 people to tell me the two or three things that were most responsible for them making $100,000 per year. I've included what they told me, because I feel that you may find it to be very valuable as you become a superstar. If you're going to emulate someone, why not emulate a winner?

The tips are given in the order that they were originally stated. I've not attempted to rate them in order of importance.

SUPERSTAR TIPS TO SUCCESS

1. Attend a Mike Ferry Action Workshop.
2. Hire a professional copywriter for fact sheets.
3. Hire a professional secretary/assistant.
4. Hire a professional CPA.
5. Use direct mailers.
6. Continually focus on visibility and networking for referrals.
7. Have a party for all of those who have given you referrals.
8. Listen to clients and then give them more than they want.
9. Practice presentation skills all the time.
10. Emulate top producers.
11. Prove on a daily basis that the client is Number One.
12. Return every call every day.
13. Be goal-oriented and analyze your goals.
14. Run your business as a business.
15. Sell your own listings.
16. Take the buyers with you when you present an offer. Have them wait in the car so that a counteroffer can be answered immediately.
17. Excel at answering objections.
18. Memorize closing techniques.
19. Don't be afraid to try something different.
20. Invest in your image and the image of your business.
21. Do not procrastinate: "What can I do to get a deal today?"
22. Make clients feel good about themselves.
23. Be a problem solver.
24. Be tenacious.

25. Prepare and present a resume on yourself to everyone.
26. Believe in yourself; "I am the best!"
27. Lead buyers and sellers by asking questions. Let them be the ones to make statements.
28. Learn the ABCs of real estate: Always Be Closing.
29. Target prospects.
30. Stay away from negative people in the office.
31. Stay focused on your goals.
32. Stay in control of clients.
33. Have a high profile in your community.
34. Give complete service.
35. Control your farm area.
36. Delegate.
37. Work long hours if you must, but always take time off each week.
38. Display large name riders on signs.
39. Make your advertising creative.
40. Obtain listings from FSBOs. Use a scripted, precise presentation.
41. Work in the more expensive market.
42. Place your own ads in the newspaper with your name.
43. Make cold phone calls.
44. Computerize yourself.
45. Have an effective and large people farm.
46. Know the difference between clients and friends.
47. Advertise yourself consistently.
48. Do the follow-up.
49. Work in a professional office.
50. Visualize, imagine and accept that you're worth a SIX-figure income.
51. Visualize the buyer and seller signing the contract.
52. Work only with people you like.
53. Give back referrals to CPAs, attorneys, tradespeople, etc.
54. Ask for a letter of reference after the deal closes.
55. Explain the process to clients carefully so that they do not get any surprises.
56. Dress professionally.
57. Get 25 centers of influence: attorneys, companies that relocate employees, etc.

58. Be persistent and enthusiastic about your goals.
59. Learn from your own mistakes.
60. Maintain a good working relationship with other agents.
61. Have a personal business history package that you give at the listing presentation.
62. Create and maintain a business image.
63. Signs—anywhere and everywhere; just keep your name in front of people.
64. Publish your own magazine. Split costs with other agents or company. Use as an insert to a newspaper.

Where do you think that the leaders in real estate come from? Are they the $10 per hour agents? No. The leaders come from the high producers; they come from the ranks of the superstars.

As you begin to produce more, you will be looked at as a role model. You will be the one aspiring superstars will want to emulate. You will become a leader.

If changes are to be made within the local board or on a national level, who do you think will be making those changes? Certainly not the $10 per hour agents—they don't have enough at stake. Besides, all they are good at is complaining. The changes are going to be brought about by you, the superstar.

If the public is to perceive real estate sales agents as professionals, the public should see professional role models. Where do you think those role models will come from? From you, the superstar.

As a superstar, you will have a lot invested in the real estate business; it's where your fortune is being made; it's where your future lies. It only makes sense that you would be interested in what happens to the business, either by legislation or by public mandate. You're going to be in a position to affect the opinions of both groups. You, like it or not, will be a leader in the industry.

Are you ready to accept the challenge of becoming a superstar? There's nothing more for me to tell you; there's no more instruction you need. I've given you the proven tools to make SIX. From the superstar profiles in the next chapter, you can see how these tools are applied on a daily basis. But you have to make the decision whether or not you're ready. It isn't enough to *think* SIX, you must *do* SIX. The question of ability does not arise; only that of desire. Do you have the desire? Are you going to become a superstar?

CHAPTER 12

Superstar Profiles

TAKING CONTROL OF MY TIME

Honore Frumentino, RE/MAX Deerfield, Deerfield, Illinois

After Honore Frumentino met Mike Ferry in 1985, she thought, "He's the first real estate trainer I've heard who uses so much common sense." At that time her annual income was $90,000. Yet Frumentino was really frustrated. "I was not in control—I was at everyone's beck and call, and not enjoying the work."

Attending Mike's seminar "probably was the turning point in my career," she recalls. Frumentino came back with plenty of ideas, and immediately implemented them. First she hired an assistant and then bought the retreat tapes "to get revived." Doing so changed her attitude about real estate. "It made me start to look at real estate as a business," she says.

It had been common for Frumentino to rush from an open house to carpool her school-age children. Yet she learned "to take control of my time in both my business and my life." In the office Frumentino will stop and appraise a situation before acting. "Before, the phone would ring and I'd go." Now she qualifies callers and turns down some listings.

A common day begins with an 8 A.M. meeting with her staff. Prospecting calls are done next. "It's the easiest thing not to get done," Frumentino explains. "So I do it before the day sweeps me away." Calls are made to FSBOs and expired listings by her prospecting assistant. A simple script is used for expireds:

> *Hello, I'm Honore Frumentino's assistant. She's a top real estate agent in Deerfield, and wants to set up an appointment to talk with you. Honore specializes in homes that should have sold and haven't.*

About half the time the expired has already relisted. Of the other 50 percent, Frumentino will end up listing about one-third.

In the afternoons prospects receive packages, and listing presentations follow in the evening. At the listing presentation, Frumentino will ask expireds if they are talking with other agents, why they listed with the company that they selected and what their previous agent did that they liked and disliked.

Two telemarketers come in the evenings and call 100 to 200 homes around new listings and sales. "They look for listings," Frumentino says, "but they'll take buyers." In addition, they call FSBOs and expired listings that the marketing assistant couldn't reach during the day.

Calling Around Listings

Frumentino has found that people are "curious and chatty" when there's a listing in the neighborhood. Her telemarketers use this script:

> *I'm calling for Honore Frumentino, one of Deerfield's top real estate agents. We just listed a home for sale in your neighborhood. Do you know anyone who would be interested in buying it? Do you want to sell in the next two years?*

When the listing is under contract, these people will be called again and informed. At that time they'll also be asked if they plan on selling within two years.

It might take ten calls, Frumentino notes, to find someone at home. Her goal is to have the office contact 100 people daily. Out of those prospects, she will get three or four leads that have long-term potential. And one lead that comes out of those calls will list within the next 30 days, she adds.

Frumentino explains that, in contrast, calling expireds and FSBOs produces results right away. Out of 20 calls, she can expect eight appointments. But it took her telemarketing venture a year to go from

Honore Frumentino uses her track record of success in this ad.

its initial startup to first closings from leads generated by the calls. A computerized tickler system reminds the telemarketers to call every few months. In addition, the callers note on the system both what they say and how the prospects respond.

Once a listing is secured, another assistant then does everything from preparing market evaluations to taking it to escrow.

Almost 60 percent of Frumentino's business comes from past clients. She keeps a mailing list of 3,000 contacts, which she mails to at least five times a year. She also rents a bus and takes her clients to a Chicago Cubs baseball game each summer.

"I'm working smarter than I've ever worked before," says Frumentino, who expects to close 100 transactions this year. "It's just as easy to take care of 35 listings as it is to handle 10 or 12, once the system's there." For instance, her computer now generates weekly update letters, whereas she used to do them by hand each Thursday.

Working with other agents also is important in getting her listings sold. Frumentino tries to "make them feel we're all part of one big team." At brokers' open houses on Tuesdays and Wednesdays she might cook lunch, have a psychic come in, or do drawings for Mike Ferry tapes. "If other agents see my name, they know the listings are in good condition and priced well," she adds.

GREAT SERVICE BRINGS REFERRALS

Dody Donahue, Century 21–Beachside REALTORS®, *Huntington Beach, California*

Dody Donahue expects to do 120 transactions this year in a market "crammed full of high-tech, high-volume producers." Donahue keeps between 30 and 70 listings, and will cancel them if they are priced too high, in order to save the costs of carrying unsaleable listings. Three-fourths of her volume comes from referrals and past clients, and the rest from prospecting.

Cultivating past clients and a people farm "cuts the cost of getting new business," Donahue notes. She explains that agents can spend less on marketing and will need to contact fewer people cold "if they work their sphere of contacts." Most of her agent referrals come from the

"Superstar 5000" network, a group of top agents who follow Mike Ferry's advice.

Providing high levels of service is important to Donahue, and her success is seen in the level of referral business she does. She has a staff of five to assist her in the following ways:

- A *transaction coordinator* does all the paperwork needed to turn listings into sales.
- A *marketing assistant* services the listings.
- A *business manager* oversees operations and helps Donahue keep her schedule.
- A *sales assistant* works with buyers and warm seller leads.
- A *telemarketer* calls cold prospects.

Aiming Higher

Donahue's sales had leveled off at $4.5 million a year when she first went to a Mike Ferry seminar in 1983. "I didn't know what to do to go higher," she remembers. Donahue had been cold calling, but after hearing Mike she started working her previous client list and calling expired listings. She also developed a "people farm" from her spheres of influence and computerized her operation. "I doubled my volume in 12 months," she adds.

What's more, Donahue's looking to get better. "If you don't keep your antenna out," she explains, "you fall behind. If you're not constantly on your toes and going back to the basics, you get lazy and sloppy. Business falls off. You have to redrill it into your skull."

Donahue says "the mega-agent of the '90s is the leader of a support team. You have to give service." To provide good service and maintain volume, her office has been redesigned and new furniture brought in to accommodate five networked computers. Everyone sits at a computer workstation, says Donahue, who first started using a computer for real estate in 1982. "There was very little real estate software," she recalls, and even though they worked with a software firm to develop a program to manage listings, escrows and accounting, it proved to be "too slow and cumbersome."

Donahue has used about half a dozen different types of software. "If there's a perfect system, I haven't found it yet," she says. Yet Donahue warns that "people who don't computerize will be left in the dust."

Lack of contact with the real estate agent is a common complaint, Donahue notes. "The average seller doesn't know a lot about real estate," she says. "Anything that goes wrong gets blamed on the agent." Her goal is that the client is still happy when the escrow is over. To that end, Donahue tries to educate clients so that "if something unfavorable happens, it has been gone over as a possible pitfall."

In addition to weekly phone contact with Donahue's office, sellers also receive newspaper articles and reports on sales in their neighborhood. "To make them know you care and are trying is half the battle," according to Donahue. "But if they don't hear from you, they assume you're doing nothing." Sellers become less demanding for open houses or other marketing efforts when there is this contact, she adds, because it helps them better understand both her efforts and the market conditions.

INCREASING PRODUCTION IN A RECESSION

Marsha Bane, Century 21 Sutherland, Arlington, Texas

Although home values have fallen in Texas over the last several years, Marsha Bane's production "has increased dramatically the last three years." She says that seeing homeowners who had to sell after losing their job or going through a divorce kept her going. "They needed me," she explains. "I went for the business."

Bane adds that "it's all in the basics—there are no gimmicks." She says that "everybody always looks for a secret, but it's a numbers game." Bane operates as a business, with a financial plan and a budget keeping her on track. "Every day I monitor listings, listing appointments, sales and prospects called. I add it up at the end of a week or a month."

While using this discipline, Bane anticipates bringing in 20 listings each month—and closing 125 deals this year. Each day Bane spends three hours calling prospects. Usually she'll call five FSBOs and five expired listings, make 50 cold calls to homes near recent sales and also call 20 past clients.

Before contacting FSBOs and expired listings, Bane provides them with information about herself and the homes she's sold, plus some reference letters. She then calls them in the evening. Each day she averages three listing appointments from these prospecting techniques.

In Bane's listing packet is a 15-minute video about her office, to which she has added a few minutes of tape on herself. A sheet of "Questions and Answers for Prospective Sellers" is included. Finally, Bane inserts disclosure statements and other forms to be filled out prior to the meeting, such as a "Ten Most Important Things about the House" sheet. Her listing presentation now runs 45 minutes to an hour, whereas it used to take two hours.

Masterminding Success

"You're competing with yourself," she explains. "There's no other competition." In fact, she relies on other agents for ideas. Each week Bane has lunch with a different "person I respect and admire" and tries to find out what makes them successful. And for the past year she has belonged to a "Mastermind Group" with 11 other superstars from around the country.

Group members take partners for ten weeks and send each other their business plan and goals for that period. Partners talk with each other several times a week to brainstorm about problems and help their counterpart stay with his or her business plan. At the end of the ten-week period the entire group meets, and members take new partners for the next ten weeks. It's a program that grew out of Mike Ferry's superstar retreats.

Bane is an active marathon runner, and she finds time to think while running six to ten miles each morning. Although she believes that it's important to brainstorm with people to work out better systems, she says that "doing what you set out to do" is the hardest part. Having a daily schedule on her desk helps keep Bane on track.

She says her two assistants "do everything." That includes taking calls, researching and writing CMAs, running ads and "paying the bills." Yet Bane notes that she hasn't yet been able to get her assistants to do prospecting calls. She prefers assistants to have a real estate license, so they can show homes to buyers. "I pay well and expect a lot," she adds.

Prospective sellers are given a form showing how the property will be marketed; open houses are not mentioned on it. "In 12 years in real estate, I've sold two homes from open houses," Bane explains. "There

Marsha Bane incorporates testimonial letters in her brochures.

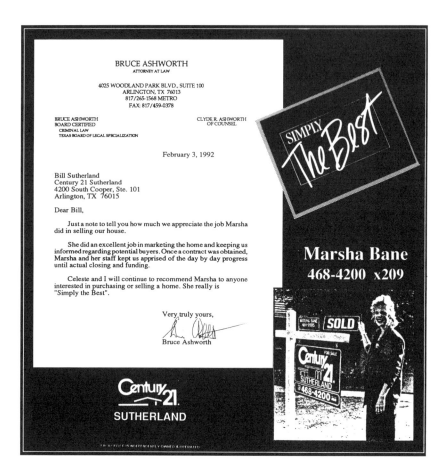

Source: Marsha Bane—Century 21 Sutherland.

are more aggressive means of selling." If the sellers insist on an open house, Bane will get someone else in her office to do it.

Setting the price right is the most important aspect of selling, she adds. Bane also does mailings to neighbors and then follows up with phone calls. Each week she mails her top ten listings to all agents in her board. Some advertising is used, and Bane also contacts prospects who have expressed interest in homes in that price range.

Her workweek lasts about 65 hours over six days each week. "I take off at least six weeks a year," she adds, and she does a lot of reading. Not overdoing it applies to her business as well. Recently Bane looked at her expenses and cut back on advertising and mailers. Doing so "hasn't affected results," she says.

LIKE A DOCTOR'S OFFICE

Froy Candelario, Superstar Realty, Arleta, California

"When I follow a plan, I can accomplish things I didn't think I could," says Froy Candelario, who will do over 200 transactions this year. Six assistants help Candelario follow up on the business he gets from knocking on 300 to 400 doors each day. In the course of a year he walks through "seven to eight cities" in Southern California, and then starts over with a new promotion.

Candelario encourages his assistants to push themselves. "I tell them it's their business, not mine. If they don't want to accomplish something, they leave." He prefers working with college students and meets with them for about 15 minutes each morning to go over what needs to be done that day. In addition, Candelario will practice scripts with them one-on-one.

A major task of the assistants is to call leads generated from Candelario's door knocking. They ask a series of questions to help qualify prospects over the phone, and Candelario has found that basically the same script can be used for buyers, sellers and expired listings:

> *When do you plan on moving?*
> *Where will you move to?*
> *Did you have a price in mind?*
> *How long have you lived here?*
> *Have you been happy here?*

When setting up an appointment for the prospect to see Candelario, the assistant will even get the lead's social security number so that a credit check can be made. Candelario's assistants include three telemarketers, one person who handles escrow matters, another who confirms appointments and a broker to ensure that the office is in compliance with all laws and regulations.

Candelario knocks on doors from 10 A.M. until four or five o'clock in the evening. Then he comes back to the office for listing appointments. One reason he has leads come to his office is so they can see that his firm is substantive. For instance, during an appointment he can call in the CPA next door, both to answer financial questions and to show prospects his resources.

Having all appointments in his office also means "I save two hours of every five by not driving."

Efficiency Means Productivity

Candelario compares his firm to a doctor's office: Prospects are shown to a room where an assistant determines their needs. Answers to questions are put on a form: How fast do you need to sell? Do you just want to get your money out, or do you have to move?

"It's very simple," Candelario explains, "and so effective." He says that 70 percent of the people who come in for appointments list with him. Candelario's presentation lasts 10 to 15 minutes. "In 30 minutes I'll do three clients," he says. Each day Candelario has ten appointments.

In addition, he sells 90 percent of his own listings. Names of prospective buyers are kept on a computer data base. Candelario's assistants look through the system, and often the home will "sell in a week or so," he says.

Each week Candelario wants to gain three listings from door knocking and four from expired listings. One approach he uses is to knock on doors around an expired listing to look for buyers. If Candelario finds one, he can go with confidence to the expired listing. His assistants also call expireds.

Not too many FSBOs are in his market. Yet when one does appear, Candelario will be in daily contact. He finds this often impresses FSBOs. "They've never seen an agent who calls on them that much," he says.

Community service also is important to Candelario. He removes graffiti and delivers ice cream to children each month. "The kids already know me," he explains. "The parents have no choice."

Candelario's goal is to complete between 240 and 260 transactions annually while working just eight hours a day. Currently he puts in 14 to 15 hours daily. Hiring an assistant to show property will allow him to meet this goal, Candelario believes. One key to staying motivated during those long hours is an exercise he does each morning. Candelario will write down his goals ten times, using statements such as "I will get four listings from expireds this week." This motivates him to go out and knock on doors.

CUTTING EXPENSES TO INCREASE PROFITS

Glenn and Saundra Pope, TRI REALTORS®, Santa Rosa, California

Saundra Pope worked traditionally when she began selling homes in 1986. "I was driving buyers around, doing listing presentations to sellers who wouldn't sell, holding open houses and taking floor time," she says. But two years later the Popes met Mike Ferry, and now they are the top agents out of 3,200 real estate salespeople in their county. Today Saundra calls expired listings and cold calls around current listings. She sends out mailers and follows up with phone calls, and she asks other superstars for referrals.

Glenn Pope concentrates on FSBOs, taking a unique approach. "Other agents beat them up," he explains. But he tells them, "I'm not here to ask for a listing; I hope you sell your house. If you do, call me if you have any questions—it's easy to make mistakes on a contract. And if you don't sell, give us a chance to help you." That initial contact will be followed up with more letters and calls. "A FSBO may take three to six months to decide to list," Glenn adds.

Prospecting expired listings is more intense; they are sent four follow-up letters in two weeks. Expireds then tend to say, "Let's at least call them," notes Saundra. She then starts asking questions, and tells them that she and her husband are the top agents in the county. Even those who don't want to talk further are sent another letter by the Popes.

Producing three appointments per day is the goal of their activity. The Popes work 60 hours from Monday through Friday. Their daily schedule looks like this:

7:30–8:30 A.M.—Call people not reached the day before.
8:30–9:00 A.M.—Meet with assistants.
9:00–11:00 A.M.—Call expired listings and FSBOs.
11:45 A.M.–12:30 P.M.—Return morning calls (no incoming calls are accepted when they are prospecting).
12:30–2:30 P.M.—Call for appointments: leads, old expireds, super-star agents (for referrals), tickler file and names on people farm.
2:30–3:00 P.M.—Return calls.
3:00–4:00 P.M.—Work out.
4:00–5:00 P.M.—Eat.
5:00–5:30 P.M.—Call for appointments.
5:30–6:30 P.M.—Present offers.
6:30–7:00 P.M.—Call people not reached earlier in the day.
7:00–9:00 P.M.—Listing appointments.

"We use Mike's scripts and his listing presentation verbatim," says Glenn. In addition, they read their goals daily to stay motivated. "Mike can be compared to a professional coach," Glenn adds, "while other trainers are more like politicians—they have more hoopla and less background. But Mike trains us to run our business properly. It's like an oriented fitness program for your business; it can withstand any market out there."

Finding Buyers

Buyers often call because of yard signs on listings. A brochure box is on the signs to provide more information. Advertising and referrals also help the Popes sell, and they note that mailings used to find listings bring out buyers. Additionally, the Popes solicit business from their list of 22,000 property owners making over $40,000 annually.

If they want to highlight a listing, they mail a flyer containing information about the home and the payments, and encouraging the prospect to call for more information. Depending on the asking price of the listing, the Popes will mail anywhere from 2,000 to 7,000 flyers. Printing and mailing 2,000 costs $560. Names of people who call to ask about the property are added to their computer list. Those prospects then will be informed about future properties that match their interests. Currently 1,700 names are kept on the computer.

Two assistants and a telemarketer help the Popes. Currently they are looking for two more telemarketers and another assistant to work with buyers. "Once you get the systems down," explains Saundra, "you can do an incredible amount of business."

But watching expenses is just as important as bringing in the deals. One year the Popes spent $150,000 in personal promotion. "Mike told us, 'You've got your name out there; now knock it off,'" remembers Saundra. To help control costs, they now have monthly profit-and-loss statements and budgets. In addition, the Popes operate on a 70/30 split system: Before it can be spent, 30 percent of their gross is put in the bank.

Whereas the Popes at one time sent out 20,000 color brochures and placed magazine ads regularly, they have reduced those efforts to a maintenance program. However, they don't cut corners on signs, believing they are the "best ad," according to Saundra. Their name rider is 20" × 24", and they use white reflective SOLD riders, which are about the same size and can be seen at night.

Working hard also cuts expenses. "Don't get lazy and rely on people to call you just because you've put out a mailer," notes Glenn. "Quit spending—get your butt out there and call."

BACK-TO-BACK APPOINTMENTS

Gladys Blum, The Prudential Real Estate Professionals,
Salem, Oregon

Before meeting Mike Ferry, Gladys Blum was doing "no prospecting. I was sitting back and letting it come to me." Still, she was closing on 100 homes a year. "He challenged me to double my production," says Blum.

Blum hired a telemarketer who makes 200 calls each night to generate leads. "And then she follows up until they are in my appointment book," adds Blum. Five to six appointments a week come from telemarketing. Two-thirds of the meetings result in a listing, she says. Most of the other prospects decide to delay selling after hearing the value of their home.

Blum handed her telemarketer Mike's trigger card and has watched her go through the entire cross-directory in a year. Last year the telemarketer helped bring in 70 listings. Blum pays her $6 per hour plus a $100 bonus at closing. In addition, calls are made to expired listings and FSBOs. Blum likes the telemarketer to get her an appointment to view a FSBO house on the first call. "It's a laid-back appointment," she explains, designed to "see if the FSBO is motivated and if I want the listing."

Transactions this year should reach 200 for Blum, who adds that it's taken her two years to double her volume. Last year she had over 170 deals. In her area, the agent closest to her production completes 80 units a year. Yet she says her hours are just "a little bit longer" than when she was closing half as many sales. Blum works from 9 A.M. to 9 P.M., six days a week.

In addition to allowing for more volume, having the right systems and assistants allows Blum to spend her time "doing more of what I love to do. My job is to be out with people, doing listing presentations and making offers."

Staying Organized

One assistant does nothing but handle transaction details, since 40 homes usually are in escrow at any one time. "Once I get an offer, I'm through with that file," says Blum. Another assistant works with buyers who have been attracted by ads, in return for 40 percent of the net. An administrative assistant handles scheduling, phones, filing and computer entry. A marketing assistant develops brochures, arranges broker open houses, handles advertising and sends letters to homes around listings.

Blum adds that "there is not much management of the assistants needed," since they've all been working together for several years. Three of Blum's assistants are licensed, and "doing better under my umbrella" than when they were listing and selling themselves. Office automation allows for greater efficiency in follow-up mailings and in generating checklists showing action required.

Because Blum has a strong reputation in the area, she can get through a listing presentation in 30 minutes. If she's not talking with a past client, she tries to determine the sellers' motivation by finding out where they are moving to and how soon they have to go. After

In this brochure, Gladys Blum touts her credentials and the teamwork of her five assistants.

Gladys...
... A great team leader

Donna Ramsey
Administrative Assistant

Connie Mitchell
Sales Assistant

Mary James
Sales Assistant

Chris Foley
Transaction Coordinator

Lucie Tisdale
Marketing Coordinator

The Prudential
Real Estate Professionals

PO Box 12397 • Salem, Oregon 97309

Phone: (503) 371-3013

When you hire Gladys, you really have six people working for you. So call today and remember, the only name you need to know in Salem real estate – *Gladys Blum*.

Gladys...
... National recognition

Today, Gladys is one of the top real estate professionals in the nation

The top residential sales associate in Salem for five years straight, she recently earned the *Top of the Rock* award – awarded to only the top ten Prudential agents in the country.

Her expertise is widely recognized in the Salem area – she even pens a weekly column called *The Real Facts* in the local newspaper.

All this translates into *real results* for her clients.

How does this soft-spoken mother of three do it?

"Honesty is of utmost importance," she says. "And once I discover what my clients' needs are, I simply put my nose to the grindstone until their goals are met."

Gladys also has a staff of five assisting her

Handling everything from advertising to computerized information systems, Gladys' staff is an experienced, well-organized team of professionals ready to serve you.

Gladys...
... A familiar face in the community

Gladys Blum

If you've lived in Salem for any length of time, it's likely that you know Gladys Blum. You might know her from church, where she teaches kindergarten through sixth grade. Or you might have met Gladys at the *Salem Executive Association* for business owners. You may have even caught one of her puppet shows that she puts on with her troop of teenage puppeteers.

But most likely, you know Gladys because she helped you

She may have helped sell your home or found a new one for you.

When Gladys began her real estate career over 12 years ago, it was a time when even experienced agents struggled. Yet she was able to carve out a loyal following who appreciate her honest, straightforward approach.

Source: Gladys Blum, The Prudential Real Estate Professionals.

Gladys
Blum

"The one name to know in Salem Real Estate"

Serving The Salem Area Market
With Knowledge, Expertise
& Compassion

The **Prudential**
Real Estate Professionals
PO Box 12397 • Salem, Oregon 97309

Phone: (503) 371-3013

Gladys...
...The Advantage

• **Listens**
Gladys takes the time to get to
know you and your individual real
estate needs before anything else.

• **Top Producer**
The fact that Gladys has been the
top sales associate in Salem for the
past five years means that you get
the results you need.

• **Service**
With a staff of five assisting her,
Gladys handles every aspect of
your transaction professionally
and promptly.

• **Results**
With over 12 years of experience
and expertise in the real estate
industry, Gladys knows how to
deliver results – time after time.
Call her today and put Salem's
top professional to work for you.

determining motivation, she presents a market evaluation and net sheet. If the prospect is interested in listing, Blum then describes the advantages she can offer. "Because I have 90 to 100 listings at all times, I have more signs out and receive more buyer calls," she says. "And I get calls from other agents constantly."

Her office is able to find buyers for her listings about 20 percent of the time. "The first four to six weeks of the listing is critical," Blum explains. During that period she sends flyers to top agents and to 100 homes surrounding the listing. However, these efforts do not include newspaper advertising. Blum says the ads "buy listings, they don't attract buyers."

But she does advertise ten to 15 homes continually on cable television. A month of weekend time costs $40, and her picture accompanies all the ads. "It's definitely useful," Blum says. A weekly column in the local newspaper also contributes to her visibility in the community. Previously she "did a lot of full-page personal promotion ads in magazines," at $400 per issue. "It gets your name out there, and you catch their eye."

Her prospecting is limited now, because "normally I have back-to-back appointments." But she does stay in touch with clients, who "keep coming back." Blum sends personal notes and a monthly newsletter to 3,300 past clients.

EARLY RETIREMENT

Kirk Kessel, The Kessel Real Estate Group, Melbourne, Florida

At age 28, Kirk Kessel already is planning his retirement. It's not too early, since he wants to begin in two years. At that point he will live off his real estate investments and start working one day per week less each year. Until then, he does 15 sales a month—although he takes off weekends and goes away for one week every 30 days. "I'd burn out without it," Kessel explains.

Prospecting is his key. Kessel and his staff make 1,000 cold calls every week—"no matter how busy you think you are." Kessel asks cold doors, "Will you be moving out in the next two years?" Because the timeframe in the question is so broad, he explains, "it knocks people off guard. They give you a friendly response," and he then can ask tougher questions:

> *Are you planning on moving in the next six months?*
> *What would make you decide to move soon?*

When making cold calls, Kessel tells prospects that he has just sold a home in their area and still has many buyers. Then he asks if they are planning on selling in the next six months. Staff assistants use the same scripts, except they begin by saying that they are calling for Kirk Kessel. "It helps to have a nonsalesperson calling," he adds. Since prospects don't perceive pressure, they are more likely to talk freely.

Yet cold calls yield just one listing per week, well short of the five he wants. Kessel needs to do ten presentations weekly to reach that goal. To help handle the volume, he has an assistant who works with each listing until it goes to contract. Another person stays with deals from the time of contract until closing. In addition, each of these staffers makes 25 cold calls a day. Kessel "treats staff people as profit centers," and will ask each one how he or she makes money. Additionally, his staff will help the office's three associate agents for a $100 per file fee.

Kessel's prospecting assistant handles incoming calls, sets up appointments and makes 100 to 125 cold calls daily. Kessel prefers to hire people with no background in the business. "If they have real estate experience," he says, "it's hard to get them out of the mode of the 1960s and 1970s real estate."

Daily Discipline

Kessel's prospecting role is to call 25 to 30 people every day, most of whom are past clients. He relies on past clients and referrals for the bulk of his business. From 7 to 9 A.M., he does office work and talks with the staff. Prospecting occurs from 9 A.M. until noon. From 1 to 4 P.M., he works with buyers and sellers and knocks on doors. Phone calls are returned and paperwork completed afterwards. In the evening Kessel does his listing presentations until 9 P.M.

He gets a listing on a little over half the presentations he makes, and walks away from prospects who won't agree to a saleable price. Kessel adds that agents "definitely compete here." But whenever he loses a listing, there isn't the disappointment agents often feel. "It's a numbers game," Kessel explains. Additionally, every day he listens to some of Mike's tapes "to stay focused and balanced."

Normally, Kessel keeps 50 to 75 listings. "I would love to have 150," he adds. When his assistant calls to set up appointments, prospects are asked if they are ready to list. Kessel's listing presentation consists first of getting all parties to agree to a price. He then explains how he markets property and gets them to sign the contract. If the prospects balk, he reminds them they've agreed on price and marketing, and asks what their question is.

When prospects say they need a day to think, Kessel fills out the paperwork and tells them he will pick it up in the morning. Or he will get them to sign the contract then, while promising to mail it back if they decide not to work with him. When sellers ask him to reduce his commission, he says, "Will you reduce your price as quickly?" During the first six weeks after listing, he wants six to ten showings and a sale. If that doesn't happen, Kessel asks for a price reduction. He says, "It's so simple. Everybody makes it so hard."

FROM $100,000 TO $400,000 INCOME IN TWO YEARS

Peter j. Sobeck, Joan m. Sobeck Inc., Hillsdale, New Jersey

Peter Sobeck had been selling homes for a dozen years—and his income had been dropping for the last five. It had fallen from $150,000 annually to $101,000 before he met Mike Ferry. For five to six months, Sobeck "was totally absorbed" in Mike's tapes and videos for five hours each day. "We're traditional agents in New England," he explains. "There's no delegating, we're not goal-oriented, we don't do high-impact prospecting and we work shorter hours."

It took some effort to start thinking differently and begin working smarter. However, a year later Sobeck's income was $300,000, and then $450,000 the following year. His production grew in a slow New England real estate market. Sobeck began looking for listings rather than buyers, tripled his support staff over six months and started calling on FSBOs and expired listings. "People I didn't normally talk to," he notes. Today half his business comes from contacting expired listings by phone.

Sixty to 70 percent of his clients are retirees. Sobeck uses a mailing list of 8,000 homeowners over age 55 for prospecting. Last year he did a lot of personal promotion to that list, although Sobeck has "curtailed that now." Advertising made an impact but was expensive. Now he relies on daily prospecting to bring in business. "You don't buy your market," he explains; "you work for it."

Four assistants work with Sobeck, "so you keep listing and selling," he says. He expects to do over 100 deals this year in an area where top producers have 12 to 15 annual transactions. Sobeck explains, "We're not trapped into doing it the old way." His one-step listing presentation lasts 30 to 40 minutes, and he delegates items such as mailings, putting up signs and lockboxes, going to closings, doing CMAs and processing listings.

What Sobeck does is spend four to five hours talking to 200 people each day by phone. If he has an appointment, that goal drops to 100 calls—and when deals are closing, he allows himself even fewer. Scripts are less necessary when calling retirees, Sobeck adds. Usually he will just say, "Do you know anyone who wants to sell their house this year?" Often he puts one of Mike's videos on low volume while he calls, and sees it over and over during the afternoon's work. To reach 200 people, it might be necessary to dial 400 or 500 times, Sobeck notes.

He's found that telemarketers produce a lead—someone expressing an interest in buying or selling—once every 40 calls. But an agent on the phone will bring in a lead for every 25 calls. FSBOs, expired listings, homes around listings, other agents and rental owners all are prospects. Sobeck also has 5,000 names on his people farm. Once that list doubles, Sobeck plans on getting all his business from referrals.

Plan for the Future

He figures that doing 150 deals a year would bring $1 million in gross commissions. In his market there are 25,000 homes, and annual turnover is 3 percent. Sobeck figures that a list of 10,000, given the turnover rate, would yield 300 transactions annually. He says he'll get half of those if they are part of his people farm.

Going after listings rather than buyers helps Sobeck control his time. But he still makes sure that listing clients "don't tell you what to do." Sobeck won't do open houses, since he sees them as a way of

Peter Sobeck shows his success where other agents have failed.

15 GOOD REASONS TO RELIST YOUR HOME WITH PETER j. SOBECK

1. The Breyer's Home: 178 Linwood Avenue, Emerson. Originally listed with Omega Real Estate for 204 days...Expired. Relisted with Remax for 120 days...Expired. **Finally listed with Peter j. Sobeck...SOLD in 8 days!**

2. The Borio's Home: 89 Kaufman Drive, Westwood. Originally listed with Murphy for 180 days...Expired. **Finally listed with Peter j. Sobeck...SOLD in 11 days!**

3. The McBrides' Home: 181 Arthur Street, Hillsdale. Originally listed with Weichert for 182 days...Expired. **Finally listed with Peter j. Sobeck...SOLD in 13 days!**

4. The Palladino's Home: 199 Howard Street, Dumont. Originally listed with Noah/Post Realtors for 180 days...Expired. **Finally listed with Peter j. Sobeck...SOLD in 13 days!**

5. The DeWeese's Home: 648 Lincoln Boulevard, Westwood. Originally listed with ERA Douglass Realtors for 261 days...Expired. **Finally listed with Peter j. Sobeck...SOLD in 15 days!**

6. The Desch's Home: 24 Emwood Avenue, Westwood. Originally listed with Schlott for 418 days...Expired. **Finally listed with Peter j. Sobeck...SOLD in 19 days!**

7. The DellaVolpe's Home: 54 East Liberty Avenue, Hillsdale. Originally listed with Coldwell Banker for 90 days...Expired. **Finally listed with Peter j. Sobeck...SOLD in 20 days!**

8. The Kokoska's Home: 267 Howard Street, Washington Township. Originally listed with Murphy for 180 days...Expired. **Finally listed with Peter j. Sobeck...SOLD in 22 days!**

Source. Peter j. Sobeck, Joan m. Sobeck, Inc., REALTORS®.

9. The Showalter's Home: 8 Edgehill Court, Woodcliff Lake. Originally listed with Weichert for 90 days...Expired. **Finally listed with Peter j. Sobeck...SOLD in 28 days!**

10. The Rimer's Home: 356 Kinderkamack Road, Hillsdale. Originally listed with Higgins Real Estate for 180 days...Expired. Relisted with Remax for 177 days...Expired. **Finally listed with Peter j. Sobeck...SOLD in 30 days!**

11. The Melber's Home: 194 Washington Street, Northvale. Originally listed with Prudential Stewart for 180 days...Expired. **Finally listed with Peter j. Sobeck...SOLD in 35 days!**

12. The Rossi's Home: 367 Piermont Avenue, Hillsdale. Originally listed w i t h Weichert for 186 days...Expired. **Finally listed with Peter j. Sobeck... SOLD in 48 days!**

13. The White's Home: 33 Woodfield Road, Washington Township. Originally listed with Coldwell Banker for 114 days...Expired. **Finally listed with Peter j. Sobeck...SOLD in 48 days!**

14. The Bradley's Home: 61 7th Avenue, Westwood. Originally listed with Koval Real Estate for 180 days...Expired. **Finally listed with Peter j. Sobeck...SOLD in 68 days!**

15. The Gluck's Home: 18 Emwood Road, Westwood. Originally listed with Coldwell Banker for 354 days...Expired. **Finally listed with Peter j. Sobeck...SOLD in 75 days!**

The above is just a <u>small</u> sampling of my sold properties. My goal is to add you to my list of success stories. My track record can't be beat!

Remember...Selling a Home is easy <u>if</u> you have the right Real Estate Broker!

Call me today...But before you do, start packing and reserve that moving van!

Peter j. Sobeck
666-1606

(The above information was compiled from data obtained through the Bergen County Multiple Lisitng Service.)

getting customers rather than a means for selling a home. "You'll end up working seven days a week" if you do them, he adds. However, at times Sobeck will have someone else put on an open house for him. Fridays and Sundays he takes off, but Sobeck is in a half-day on Saturdays. "The work is productive," he says. Since Sobeck doesn't work with buyers, he "rarely previews homes." Instead, buyer leads are offered to another agent for a referral fee.

DOING MORE THAN I EVER THOUGHT POSSIBLE

Karen Bernardi, RE/MAX Realty Consultants, Boulder, Colorado

"It's just as easy to make a lot of money as to make a little," says Karen Bernardi. "You work just as hard either way." Although she was "one of the top three or four agents in town" before meeting Mike Ferry, her income jumped by 75 percent immediately after hearing him. "I quit farming and taking floor time," says Bernardi. A year later, her income had doubled. "I schedule my day as Mike instructs," she adds.

"A lot of agents show up and hope it happens," Bernardi continues. "But when you actively prospect for people, it becomes a science, not luck." She thinks that many agents aren't as businesslike in their approach, because "most of us got into real estate by default. We didn't want to be a real estate agent as a child."

Bernardi adds that heavy prospecting "is uncomfortable. You get more rejection—and you also get more success. But it's hard to change."

One reason she was willing to change was her awareness that selling real estate isn't the same as it used to be. "The cost of doing business is going up," Bernardi explains, citing the price of advertising, mailing and printing. "You have to do more volume" to make a profit, she notes, and adds that sellers want both more marketing work done and more contact with an agent.

"Agents spend too much time doing $5 an hour work," she explains. "Typing, filing, delivering things, cutting and pasting, and making labels. Getting brochures printed is not work." Bernardi notes that "all my staff make more than the average agent does."

She suggests agents hire a part-time assistant. "You can't afford not to," she says. Bernardi's seven assistants free her to spend all her time prospecting, presenting contracts and listing houses. As a result, she expects to sell 200 homes this year. Three telemarketers, three full-time assistants and one part-time helper make up Bernardi's staff. In addition, another person does her deliveries.

When Bernardi's telemarketers cold call, they make sure to tell the prospect that the market's great and that they just sold a house; then they ask if he or she plans on selling in the next year or two.

Out of every 100 persons contacted, Bernardi gets one listing. Thirty to 40 prospects are contacted each hour, and the goal is to generate seven leads in one three-hour evening shift.

Most of the leads are from people whose plans to sell are not immediate. The following day, Bernardi's prospecting coordinator calls each lead to set up an appointment. At listing presentations, Bernardi says she "does Mike's script." Her first question is, "Are you planning on listing your home with me tonight?" Bernardi adds that she "rarely loses a listing. I get 29 out of 30 that I want."

Personal Prospecting

Bernardi doesn't rely on her staff alone to get leads. "I knock on doors every day," she says. "We're selling 20 homes a month, so you usually can say, 'We just sold a house in your neighborhood.'" However, over half of her volume comes from repeat business and referrals. Bernardi sends out mailings twice a month, which amounts to "a big expense." She also calls the 700 people on her "listed or sold" list—as well as contacting friends—every three months.

Volume in the first four months of this year equaled Bernardi's total production of two years ago. "Mike expanded my vision. I'm doing more than I ever thought was possible." She notes that half her gross income goes to expenses, including car costs. Yet Bernardi adds that "expenses are not up proportionally" to the sales increase that's occurred since hiring the staff.

Bernardi prefers that staffers have no real estate background and "be not necessarily like me. If they were like me, then I might get a salesperson, not an assistant." She also encourages herself and the staff by setting goals for the office. For instance, she might tell the staff that if 50 homes are sold in the next two months, they'll all go to Las Vegas for a weekend. "I'm not good at long-term goals," Bernardi explains, so she looks two months ahead at most.

To help get those homes sold, she does mailings to 20 houses on each side of the listing. Bernardi also mails to past clients and leads. Her workweek ranges from 55 to 60 hours. However, "I take a lot of vacations," she says. "I travel about two months out of the year"—going to places such as the Red Sea and South America.

EFFECTIVE ADVERTISING TO FIND BUYERS

John MacCorkindale, Professionals 100, Beaverton, Oregon

John MacCorkindale is different from most superstars, since "76 percent of my volume comes from sales. Instead of prospecting for listings, I have been prospecting for buyers." Right now he is working "to get more listings without losing buyers."

He says that "massive amounts of advertising" are used to get calls from people looking to purchase. "If you advertise generically and appeal to what people want, they will respond." For instance, if the economy is slow, MacCorkindale will run ads with headlines such as "Affordable Homes," or "Cheaper than Rent."

Following those "eye-catcher" statements, his ads provide a minimal amount of information in order to encourage buyers to call him. MacCorkindale makes sure the ad has "enough closing to get a call."

For instance, an ad might have the headline "Starter Homes." Underneath, MacCorkindale would describe four houses with prices ranging from $67,000 to $94,000. At the bottom he would tell them to "Call John MacCorkindale." Another ad would read, "Attention Investors—Assumable Loans," and then describe duplexes and four-plexes ranging in price from $49,000 to $79,000. Different areas would be mentioned "generically" in these "conceptual ads speaking to what the market wants." At least a third of the buyers MacCorkindale works with are investors, he adds.

Half of the 300 phone calls he gets each month come on Sundays, in response to the ads. MacCorkindale says that's a better result than he would get from making 3,000 cold calls. When the phone rings, he responds with a series of qualifying questions. "We qualify very hard,"

MacCorkindale says. Even so, "we get fooled sometimes." His qualifying process includes the following questions:

- *Which ad are you calling about?* (in order to find out which ads work the best)
- *What is your name?*
- *What is your phone number?*
- *What area are you interested in?*
- *How large a house are you looking for?*
- *How big is your down payment?*
- *Is your credit good?*
- *How long have you been looking for a home?*
- *Are any agents helping you?*
- *How soon do you need to buy?*

To avoid spending time driving buyers around, MacCorkindale gives the addresses of three to five homes for the prospects to look at by themselves. He calls prospects after they've driven by the homes—and makes sure to requalify them during every phone conversation. If they're interested in one of the homes, MacCorkindale arranges a showing, then determines if the prospects want to make an offer.

FSBO Strategy

MacCorkindale is beginning to prospect FSBOs for listings. His technique in approaching these prospects is unique. Currently Mac-Corkindale has 40 listings, though he wants to have between 50 and 100.

Since 7 percent commissions are the rule in Oregon, MacCorkindale feels as though he can offer a discount to pick up more business. When calling FSBOs, the telemarketers will say,

Hello, I'm calling for John MacCorkindale, the top-selling agent in Portland. He can sell your home for a lower fee.

When the FSBO asks about the fee, he or she is told that it is 6 percent if two brokers are involved, 4 percent if MacCorkindale finds a buyer and 2 percent if the FSBO finds a buyer. The caller closes by telling the FSBO that he or she will receive service and a faster sale. "Doesn't that make sense?" is the ending.

"They're simple scripts and have predictable results," adds Mac-Corkindale. He says that 25 to 35 percent of those reached by phone want a package or a presentation from him. About 10 percent of the prospects who get to this stage eventually list with MacCorkindale, who hopes to get 15 FSBO listings a month. During the week his assistants and telemarketers call FSBOs, and MacCorkindale follows up the leads.

Up to seven letters will be sent to FSBOs, and a schedule of calls is followed. MacCorkindale finds they often list after 30 days. He is so excited about this market that one person has been hired part-time to drive around town and look for FOR SALE BY OWNER signs. MacCorkindale tried this himself, and in 90 minutes found 20 FSBOs that weren't advertising in the newspaper. His driver is paid $5 per hour plus gas money.

However, over 80 percent of his business during the last four to five years has come from advertising. MacCorkindale anticipates 150 transactions this year. "I'm looking for investors who will buy several properties a year and list with me when they sell." In that way he will "get it back as a listing in the next two to five years."

MacCorkindale also contacts people with property to rent and asks them if they'd like "to sell their home for a lower fee." In addition to offering the lower fee schedule, at times MacCorkindale will offer a guarantee that if the seller isn't happy, he or she can cancel the listing in 30 days.

WE DOUBLED PRODUCTION IN NINE MONTHS

Kim and Daryl Rouse, RE/MAX Real Estate Specialists, Long Beach, California

Each year Kim and Daryl knock on 50,000 doors. "Our goals are bigger than the obstacles," says Kim. At times Daryl will walk through neighborhoods for up to six hours in a day to reach his goal of talking to 150 people. Over a third of the Rouses' 150 transactions this year will come from this prospecting. Kim and Daryl knock on doors in areas where recent sales have been strong.

Daryl has several scripts to draw on but likes to start with an open-ended question that is hard to say "no" to. Often he will simply ask—

When do you plan on moving?

Daryl then might ask some questions to put the conversation on a friendly basis, such as—

How long have you lived here?
How did you pick this area?
If you were planning to move, where would you go?

And then he asks—

When would that be?

Anyone who says they're planning to move within the next two years is a lead for the Rouses. Leads are immediately sent a letter of thanks for their time, and their names go into the computer system. Each month they get a letter, and there is regular phone contact. "Often their needs change," explains Kim. "If they say they want to sell in two years, they usually do so within one year."

She adds that there may be 25 contacts with a lead before they decide to list. Currently they have 2,200 leads, and a telemarketer follows up on them. After a while the telemarketer gets to know the prospects and calls with information that's beneficial to them:

I'm touching base with you on behalf of Kim and Daryl Rouse. Interest rates are dropping (or sales are picking up in your area). Are your plans still the same concerning moving?

Sellers are looking for "someone they can trust, and someone they feel is competent," says Kim. To convey that image, the Rouses describe their track record and show testimonial letters from people in that neighborhood.

Although they portray themselves as a team, the Rouses don't knock on doors or go to listing presentations together. Instead, they work different sides of the street, and either one will take the listing appointment. Working separately makes them more efficient. "People aren't necessarily looking for a warm feeling," Kim says. "They are looking for someone competent." However, the Rouses have a personal

Kim and Daryl Rouse make the most of their publicity by reprinting it in handouts.

Home buyer's kit assembled by the Rouses

Kim and Daryl Rouse of RE/MAX* Real Estate Specialists have assembled a free kit to assist those in the market for a home.

The kit includes a free 60-minute audio cassette of tips.

"Our buyer's kit is not only for the first-time buyer, but also contains information useful to the more sophisticated reinvestment buyers of homes," Daryl Rouse says.

"We have carefully edited our information package so that it is both helpful and easy to understand," according to Kim Rouse.

To receive a home buyer's kit, call and make an appointment with Kim or Daryl at (213) 985-3240.

Kim and Daryl are the top listing and sales agents for this year at RE/MAX* Real Estate Specialists.

For more information on buying or selling, please call
Kim & Daryl
at
(213) 985-3240.

Reprinted from a recent article in the Press Telegram.

brochure that tells more about themselves, so that prospects can feel as though they know the couple.

Finding Buyers

Three-fourths of their business comes from sellers, and the Rouses sell about 40 percent of those themselves. Door knocking also helps uncover buyers, and their assistants cold call lists of renters who make over $40,000 and have good credit. The callers say that they have homes for sale in that area and ask renters if they know how easy it is to buy.

Each prospect is encouraged to come in for an appointment and is sent material through the mail. In fact, the Rouses keep up the contact "until they tell us not to call five or six times in a row." Some prospects take a long time to get ready—Kim notes they've put 10,000 leads on the computer system over the last two years, numbering them consecutively. Recently number 57 bought a home.

Two assistants and one full-time and two part-time telemarketers make up their staff. The Rouses suggest that agents split an assistant with another salesperson at first in order to be able to afford one. "Within nine months after we started using assistants we doubled production," says Kim. "It's gone up steadily since then." In fact, their production doubled "when the market was heading south," she adds. "Had we not met Mike when we did, we probably would have been a casualty of the market."

MARKETING YOURSELF AND YOUR LISTINGS

Erica West, RE/MAX Fountain Hills, Fountain Hills, Arizona

Each year anywhere from 300 to 350 homes sell in Fountain Hills, which is outside Phoenix. Erica West expects to sell over 30 percent of them this year. "I have a really good market share," she explains.

If it sounds as if West has celebrity status, that isn't far from the truth. Once a month she is on the CBS affiliate station's noon television news show. For two or three minutes West discusses a real estate topic.

She might explain why title insurance is necessary or talk about interest rates—and she also takes call-in questions.

West was selling just 40 homes annually when she met Mike three years ago. Since then she has hired two full-time and one part-time assistant. "My priority is to be with a buyer or a seller at all times, and leave the rest to assistants," West says.

Mike impressed on her that "you have to run it like a business," she notes. "Homes are my inventory—I have to fill my shop with homes I know will sell." West's husband works with prospective buyers who respond to ads, and in that way they sell at least 40 percent of their own listings.

Marketing System

West writes her own marketing copy—a task she enjoys, since she is a former language arts teacher. Her marketing program for listings includes the following:

1. Ads are placed in the local newspaper and regional magazine. West notes that advertising costs less in her small town than it does in larger cities, so the exposure her properties receive is worth the expense.
2. Brochures are used to reach different prospects. West notes that "there are three ways people buy: through an agent, from driving by the property and from reading ads. I want to approach them all."

Consequently, she prepares a color brochure that is mailed to agents and prospective buyers who call to ask about the listing. A stack is left in the home for the showing agents as well. Finally, black and white copies of the brochure are stapled to a "Guide to Homes" flyer that shows all her listings. It then is put in the brochure box on West's sign in front of each listing. Persons who become interested when driving by can pick up a brochure and be exposed to all her listings.

3. A "REALTOR®-to-REALTOR® Highlights" flyer that describes West's best listings is mailed to 400 agents outside the community. In addition, she hand-delivers 100 copies to local real estate salespeople in order to maintain personal contact and "to combat the jealousy" stemming from her success.

4. Postcards describing the listed home are mailed to 100 to 150 homes in the neighborhood. West puts her picture on the front of the postcard, just as she does with all her other marketing materials.

About $300 to $350 is spent marketing each listing, says West, which amounts to 12 percent of her gross commissions. Many of the tasks are carried out by one of West's assistants, who works from a checklist to make sure everything is done. West adds that her second assistant handles clerical work.

Prospecting is done by calling homeowners from the cross-directory. Often West picks a street with homes she knows will attract buyers. West adds that hiring telemarketers isn't as effective in a small town as in other places. Because she is well-known, homeowners want to talk directly with her. To reinforce this personal touch, West's part-time weekend assistant addresses envelopes by hand while answering the phone.

Marketing is important to West. "If you can't learn to market yourself, how are you going to market properties?" she asks. West recalls that at one time there was just a single grocery store in Fountain Hills. She gained great publicity by spending $2,000 to put an ad on the front of each grocery cart for six months. West also hired a public relations representative to help get her on television. She still retains that person to write press releases.

Persistence and attention to detail help West in all aspects of the business, not just marketing. For instance, she also sells homes about to go into foreclosure. West might convince the lender that it's better to get a home sold and lose a little money than it is to take back the house keys. Bankers have started approaching West for help on their problem real estate loans now. But she adds that it requires "a lot of follow-up" to make this strategy successful.

Erica West provides this list of questions to sellers who will be interviewing other agents.

A SELLERS GUIDE
to interviewing a real estate
agent to sell your property

1. Do you work as a full time Realtor?

2. Do you have a full-time personal assistant?

3. What area & in what aspect of the market do you specialize.

4. Do you have a written marketing plan specifically designed to selling my house?

5. Do you attend the Realtor's Board Meeting? How often?

6. How do you market properties directly to buyers?

7. How many properties have you sold in the last 3 months?

8. Will you produce a professional flyer of my home with picture displaying my home?

9. What publications will you advertise my home in? How often?

10. How often will I hear from you after my home is listed with you?

11. How will you let me know what you are doing to market my property?

12. How do you find potential buyers?

13. What other marketing techniques will you use to get my property sold?

14. In what ways do you encourage other realtors to sell my property?

15. How do you help me prepare my home for sale?

16. How confident are you that you can sell my home at full price? Why?

17. How many listings do you have? What percentage of them sell?

It will probably not come as a big surprise to you that I believe I am the best choice to get your property sold. However, regardless of your decision the questionnaire should prove helpful.

RE/MAX fountain hills
13253 la montana drive, suite 102
fountain hills, arizona 85268
office: (602) 837-3373, 1-800-447-9016
an independent member broker

Source: Erica West, RE/MAX Fountain Hills, Arizona.

INDEX